50 Ways
to Fight
Censorship

50 Ways to Fight Censorship

and Important Facts to Know About the Censors

by Dave Marsh
and Friends

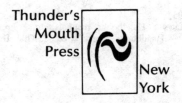

Thunder's
Mouth
Press

New
York

Published by Thunder's Mouth Press
54 Greene Street, Suite 4S
New York, NY 10013

Library of Congress cataloging-in-publication data:

Marsh, Dave.
    50 ways to fight censorship : and important facts to know about the censors / by Dave Marsh. — 1st ed.
        p.   cm.
    Includes index.
    ISBN 1-56025-011-9 : $5.95
    1. Censorship — United States — Handbooks, manuals, etc. 2. Freedom of information — United States — Handbooks, manuals, etc. I. Title. II. Title: Fifty ways to fight censorship.
Z658.U5M37   1991   91-3209
363.3'1'0973—dc20   CIP

Text design by Ed Hedemann
Typeset by Royal Type
Manufactured in the United States of America

For the little kid who's keepin' it hid:
Keep that radio under your pillow
tuned in to your dreams

CONTRIBUTORS

Danny Alexander

Bill Ayres

Lee Ballinger

James Bernard

Rachel Burd

David Cantwell

Sandra Choron

Greg Drew

Thom Duffy

Zoë Edelen

Ben Eicher

Allen Ginsberg

Michael "Supe" Granda

Karen Hall

Brian Keizer

Noah Kimerling

Mary Morello

Steve Perry

Phyllis Pollack

Henry J. Rich

Luis J. Rodriguez

Mike Stark

John Waters

Daniel Wolff

John Woods

ACKNOWLEDGMENTS

This is an angry book, a book about getting so fed up you start to take action in the hope of changing the world. But if it's any good at all, that's because it was written and compiled with love — love for the freedoms we cherish and more particularly, for those who have helped keep those freedoms alive.

Books are important because they are grounded in ideas. The idea for this one came from my agent, Sandra Choron, who also contributed, as she always does, in several other ways. On behalf of First Amendment supporters everywhere, I thank her with all my heart.

Many publishers had the opportunity to support this idea. Neil Ortenberg and his staff at Thunder's Mouth Press were the ones brave enough to do so. Neil, Anne Stillwaggon, Jean Casella, Eric Brandt, Janey Tannenbaum, and the rest of the Thunder's Mouth folks always publish good and important books, in many cases the kind the censors would love to get their claws on, and I'm proud to join their list. Special mention should be made of two interns, Henry J. Rich and Zoë Edelen, who did much of the hard work of tracking down names, addresses, dates, and places. Henry in particular deserves great praise for his diligence and creativity, particularly in the sections he helped compose on voting and the movies. A third intern, Marian Cole, was a resourceful and tireless fact-checker. Joan Fucillo's copyediting of the book was both exacting and sensitive. Ed Hedemann, Rusty Hoover, and Wileda Wasserman were integral to the production process.

The other contributors responded to the call to create this book quickly (almost all of it was written between Labor Day and Thanksgiving, 1990) and with all their might. Some contributed ideas and suggestions; some did research; some wrote material that was combined with my own words. As this project's Tom Sawyer, I thank them all for helping me paint this fence, and paint it well. Extra attention goes to Danny Alexander and David Cantwell, for writing the basic text for several sections, based on their experiences teaching and free-speeching in the Midwest; Mary Morello, for her insights into grassroots organizing; Bill Ayres, for creating the basic material on news and political censorship; Brian Keizer, who did much of the writing for the book's final two sections; Daniel Wolff, who did much of the research and writing on libraries; and James Bernard, for his writing on how to deal with the media. Phyllis Pollack contributed both writing and research from her seemingly bottomless knowledge of all that's worst about the censors. My *Rock & Roll Confidential* partner of many years, Lee Ballinger, operated out beyond the edge of comradeship, contributing ideas, research, and writing, adding editorial insight, and keeping a keen eye for the main goals. A number of friends in the freedom-fighting trade offered indispensable succor: Richard Bray of PEN Center West, a great friend in many struggles and the person who first introduced me to Thunder's Mouth Press; Judy Krug of the ALA's Freedom to Read Foundation; Oren Teicher at the ABA; and Barry Lynn of the ACLU. These men and women are the most dangerous day-to-day opponents that censors in America have. I hope that the words on these pages, and the actions that stem from them, will form the sort of tribute that they deserve.

CONTENTS

Foreword by George Plimpton ix
Introduction xv
What Is Censorship? 1
Ten Commandments for the Fight Against Censorship 2

50 WAYS TO FIGHT CENSORSHIP

1. Speak Out! 5
2. Register and Vote! 7
3. Send Your Senators and Congressperson Letters or Mailgrams . 10
4. Teach Your Children How to Know When Censorship Appears in
   the Classroom, or Elsewhere 13
5. Oppose De Facto Censorship of the News Media by the Wealthy
   and Powerful 17
6. Get Involved With Your Library 21
7. Make Art That Fights Censorship 24
8. Speak Out About Freedom of Speech at Schools, Churches, and
   to Youth Groups in Your Town 26
9. Write a Letter to Your Local Paper in Defense of Free Speech . . 28
10. Call Your Radio Station Talk Show 29
11. Support Those Retailers Who Fight Against Censorship 31
12. Read Everything You Can Get Your Hands On About Censorship
    and First Amendment Issues; Read Banned Books 35
13. Gather Information and News Clippings on Censorship and Send
    Them to a Central Clearinghouse 42
14. Buy Banned Records, Fight Record Labeling 43
15. Write and Perform Songs About Free Speech and the Perils of
    Censorship 44
16. Write Movie Moguls and Tell Them to Eliminate the MPAA
    Ratings Code 47
17. Watch "The Simpsons" and Other Controversial TV Programs . 51
18. Contact Your Local Cable Outlet to Find Out if It's Being
    Pressured to Censor Its Programming 56
19. Join the American Civil Liberties Union 57
20. Join the Freedom to Read Foundation 59
21. Stop the Attack on the National Endowment for the Arts 60
22. Join Article 19 63
23. Support the American Booksellers Association Foundation for
    Free Expression 64
24. Get to Know the Censorship Groups, Study Their Literature,
    and Expose Them to Public Scrutiny 65

25. Investigate the Tax-Exempt Status of Pro-Censorship Lobbying
    Groups 71
26. Find Out Your State's Requirements for Purchasing Textbooks . 72
27. Run for Office on a Platform Supporting Freedom of Expression . 75
28. Write to Your Favorite Artists; Find Out What They're Doing to
    Help Preserve Freedom of Expression 78
29. Make an Anti-Censorship Home Video Showing the Various
    Benefits of Free Speech in Your Community 82
30. Write About Your Positive Experiences With Art 83
31. Become a Voter Registrar; Organize a Voter Registration Drive . 87
32. Form a Group That Establishes a First Amendment Litmus
    Test for Politicians 89
33. Start an Anti-Censorship Petition Campaign 91
34. Boycott Products Made and Marketed by Companies That Fund
    the Censors 92
35. Start a Grassroots Anti-Censorship Organization 93
36. Start an Anti-Censorship Newsletter 95
37. Contact Local Arts and Educational Groups; Persuade Them to
    Stage a Free Speech Event 97
38. Set a Good Example — Start a Parents Group to Combat
    Censorship 99
39. Contact Local TV Stations and Propose a "Censored Films
    Festival" 99
40. Use Community Access Cable TV or Community Radio to Raise
    Awareness of Free Speech Issues 101
41. Create a Public Service Announcement to Be Aired Over the
    Radio 104
42. Stage a Mock Trial on Censorship 104
43. Make Sure Local Schools Have a Course on Freedom of Speech . 105
44. Contact Others Concerned About Censorship — Put It in the
    Want Ads! 107
45. Talk to Teachers About What They're Doing to Ensure Free
    Speech 108
46. Picket the Censors 109
47. Sue the Bastards! 110
48. Have a Moment of Silence to Keep Speech Free 112
49. Organize a Speak Out Day 113
50. Make the Real Obscenities the Real Issues 115

Afterword by Barney Rosset 118
Index 121

FOREWORD

The summer 1990 issue of the literary quarterly the *Paris Review* included a letter, signed by the publisher Deborah Pease, to the National Endowment for the Arts, turning down its $10,000 grant to the magazine — an act taken because she and the editors did not feel they could countenance the restrictions required before receiving the grant. The letter reiterated the magazine's gratitude to the Endowment for its help in the past, as well as its dismay that the Endowment's survival apparently depended on caving in to its enemies.

The publisher used the word *dismal* in her assessment of the atmosphere in which the Endowment and its beneficiaries find themselves, and that seems to me quite accurate. We have gone through such times of restrictions before. I thought our readers might be interested if I described some of them.

In the early days when the magazine was printed abroad, it was the U.S. Customs we had to worry about. We dealt with a Mr. Demcy, the "Censor." I wrote about him in the short history of the magazine which appears in the 25th anniversary issue of the *Review*:

> His office was on Varick Street. The desk down from him was occupied by the Customs official who specialized in woolen goods. Mr. Demcy's field was literature. Danish nudist magazines lay on top of his desk. His judgement as to whether these were obscene was a simple one: if pubic hair showed, pornographic! The only nudist magazines which could be admitted into the country were those which had been airbrushed, so that the offending areas of women playing volley-ball had taken on the alabaster sheen and innocence of children's dolls.
>
> When I returned to New York in 1956, I would regularly visit Mr. Demcy to discuss the contents of a newly arrived issue . . . which would not be allowed off the docks until Mr. Demcy had given his okay. We would argue about what was obscene. Mr. Demcy, who read each issue from cover to cover, had a theory that since there was no legally workable definition of obscenity, each case "stood on its own merits," and that if prurient the material might endanger a "young person" or what Mr. Demcy called a "susceptible reader."
>
> Thus, there was a great deal of discussion in the musty office on Varick Street about the typical *Paris Review* subscriber and his possible "susceptibility." Mr. Demcy agreed that the *Paris Review* reader probably would not be depicted on the cover of the *Saturday Evening Post* ("Not a typical Norman Rockwell, if you know what I mean," he once said) but that nonetheless the subscribers might well be family people with youngsters who could happen upon a copy of the magazine and get to browsing through it.
>
> I, on the other hand, provided a counter-portrait — a crag-faced subscriber who was a fusty ex-professor living alone in a made-over

Vermont barn, working on a novel about patricide, a writer-manqué who subscribed to the *Review* only to verify that his own stuff was better than what was being published; as soon as he had done with it, he smugly tossed the magazine into the Franklin stove.

A great falling out with Mr. Demcy occurred with the *Paris Review* #21, which arrived on the New York docks on the eve of the longshoremen's strike. I pleaded with Mr. Demcy to let the issue through Customs before everything closed down. I assured Mr. Demcy, who had not seen an advance copy, that nothing in the issue would outrage the sensibilities of the Customs official's hypothetical "reader." I did not mention a story by Alex Trocchi, an excerpt from his novel, *Cain's Book*, in which a few formidable expletives appeared. I knew of them, of course, but they seemed so proper to the context of the story and its characters that I surmised that even Mr. Demcy would appreciate their appropriateness.

I was wrong. Mr. Demcy let the crates of *Paris Review* off the docks but in checking a copy the next day, he ran across the line, "Give me that spike quick or I'll slit your fucking throat!" (To find this, a single line, in a magazine of almost 200 pages of print and poetry suggests how zealously Mr. Demcy tried to protect his constituency.) In a rage he telephoned me. How dare I say that there was nothing salacious in the issue? Why, what about this "slitting throat" line in the Trocchi story (Mr. Demcy could not bring himself to say the offending word)? He went on to say that the next morning he was sending the U.S. marshals out to bond the issue. Most likely it would end up being burned on the city dump. Where was it?

I refused to tell him. I asked Mr. Demcy if he had read the T.S. Eliot interview in the same issue. Was it not fine? Mr. Demcy was not placated. Where were the copies? Again, I would not say. Mr. Demcy hung up. Since the crates were in the distribution company's warehouse, which Mr. Demcy might well guess, and dispatch his marshals there, I led a crew of *Review* people to the warehouse that evening; a number of the crates were spirited away to various cellars in the Village.

Eventually the proper authorities in Washington reviewed the issue #21 and determined that it was not anything that should end up in the city dump. The subscribers eventually got their copies. Thereafter, the gap between the antiquated codes of Customs and those of the U.S. mails, whose censorship authority had been so drastically changed by the implications of various court cases, especially *Roth v. the United States* in 1957, became indistinguishable; the *Review* never had to deal with Mr. Demcy again.

He retired in 1965. He was very proud of a book he published during his years with the Customs people. It was entitled, *How To Cope With United States Customs* — dedicated to his mother, whose name was Reggie. I received an inscribed copy.

I have always wondered what Mr. Demcy would have made of a strange case involving the *Paris Review* which occurred a decade later. At a John Birch Society meeting at a library in South Farmingdale, Long Island, a member of that ultra–right wing organization sitting in the back row leaned back in his chair and removed by chance a copy of the *Paris Review* from the shelves. Somewhat to the discomfort of the evening's featured speaker, I would have thought, he began browsing through it (issue #38). He was horrified by what he came across in a story by Dallas Wiebe entitled "Skyblue at the Dump" — namely by a lyrical description of a rather dowdy schoolteacher (her head spinning with visions of the miscegenative acts in the Greek myths) being made love to by a bull. Removing the copy from the library (apparently with some difficulty because a charge of third-degree assault was made by a woman librarian), the aggrieved testified later at his trial for petty larceny that he had done so "to alleviate what I felt to be an immanent threat to the moral welfare of my children." An echo of Mr. Demcy's worries! The jury did not agree this gave him the right to remove the magazine; it took only 28 minutes to find him guilty.

About this time (the late '60s) I began to have problems of my own with a National Endowment project eventually entitled *The American Literary Anthology*. Roger Stevens, the first Endowment head, had called me in to devise a program to help the literary magazines and their contributors. The plan was to publish an annual volume of the best work — fiction, poetry, essays — selected from the country's magazines. National Endowment funds were to be used not only for publication costs but to pay contributors — $1,000 for prose material, $500 for each poem, and to reward the magazine ($250) in which the work first appeared. It was a sensible concept — a simple way of fulfilling what writers, especially those making no compromise with public taste, hope to get from their labors . . . recognition, distribution, and compensation. My own involvement was to oversee the project.

For the second volume of the *Anthology*, the panel of judges selected a poem by Aram Saroyan. An example of the "calligraphic" form with which he was experimenting at the time, the poem in its entirety only had seven letters ("Lighght"). Its brevity caught (and held!) the eye of a congressman from Iowa, William Scherle, an arch-critic of the National Endowment and its programs. The fact that American taxpayers had paid $500 for Saroyan's effort, along with $250 to the editor of the *Chicago Review* where the poem had appeared, outraged him. The poem was not pornographic or blasphemous; it was too *short*! Scherle flailed away on the floor of the Congress. He referred to me as a "dilettante." Editorial and letter columns had a field day. Readers sent in caustic and even shorter imitations of "Lighght". I remember traveling to Washington in the forlorn hope of explaining to Scherle the importance of "little magazines," their function in the literary community, their importance, and perhaps even an explanatory word or two about "calligraphic" poetry. Alas, no luck. He wouldn't see me. I remember an aide proudly pointing out an "artwork" in the anteroom — a painting of an Iowa corncob done by a woman who had lost control of her limbs and had done the job "with just the use of her teeth."

How did the Endowment behave on this occasion? "Frightened," was my opinion at the time, pretty much what it is today watching the Endowment knuckling under — however practical the solutions — to such William Scherle clones as Pat Robertson and Jesse Helms. The support of the *Anthology* program was soon dropped — the first indication I can recall suggesting the Endowment felt public taste and reaction should be a determinant in the awarding of grants.

The problem always has been that the relationship between government authorities (representing the public, of course) and the arts is an uneasy one at best. Blasphemy, pornography, have been the sticking points. And politics. During the Depression the New Deal's Federal Writers' Project benefited thousands of writers (none receiving more than $100 a month, incidentally) and resulted in hundreds of books and pamphlets; it was extinguished after eight years, mainly by the efforts of the Martin Dies Committee, convinced that the Project guidebooks were vehicles for left-wing propaganda. What a circus *that* was! A Congressman Starnes on the Committee attacked Hallie Flanagan, a Project director, for praising the Russian theater as "live and vital." He persisted by quoting a phrase from an article she had written, "Marlowesque Madness."

"Who is this Marlowe?" he wanted to know. "Is he a Communist?" Mrs. Flanagan explained that she meant Christopher Marlowe. Starnes, who had apparently never heard of Marlowe, asked Mrs. Flanagan to "tell us who Marlowe is." Mrs. Flanagan asked that it be put on record that Marlowe was "the greatest dramatist in the period of Shakespeare, immediately preceding Shakespeare." A shout of laughter went up which apparently silenced Starnes, but only for the rest of the session.

I can never consider these matters without recalling Ralph Ginzburg's frightening experience in the 1960s. He was the editor of *Eros* — a beautifully designed magazine with a hard cover, no advertising, and slick pages. Its contents were relatively highbrow, and its illustrative work certainly mild by today's standards — nude photographs of Marilyn Monroe, tasteful photographic studies in black and white of a black male and a white woman, both nude. (Ginzburg has wondered since if his problems would have lessened if the sexes in those photographs had been reversed.)

What in fact got Ginzburg into trouble was not so much the material selected for his magazine but that he made enquiries of the post offices of two small villages in Pennsylvania with the improbable names of Intercourse and Blue Ball (the four hamlets, Bird In Hand, Intercourse, Paradise, and Blue Ball, are linked in a row on Route 340 in Central Pennsylvania) asking if they could handle a mailing drive for *Eros*. How appropriate to have the postmarks on their solicitations! The post office people in Intercourse and Blue Ball were not disrespectful. They replied that their post offices were no more than siderooms off a grocery store; they simply couldn't handle the enormous mailing drive Ginzburg had in mind.

The mere suggestion of doing this rather clever, if not charming, promotion ran afoul of the pandering prohibitions implicit in *Roth v. U.S.* A federal matter, the Attorney General's Office initiated proceedings. So did the fact that Ginzburg's regular mailing outlet was Middlesex, New Jersey, milder in innuendo than the Pennsylvania hamlets but with a post office capable of mailing out 120,000 copies of *Eros*. The contents of *Eros* #4 also raised federal hackles — a feature entitled "Love in the Bible" (Rembrandt illustrations), an article on female impersonators, an Allen Ginsberg photo of a naked woman viewed at a distance from the rear, selections from Frank Harris's *My Life and Loves*, an article by a *Time* senior editor entitled "Was Shakespeare a Homosexual?", a collection of bawdy limericks, etc., etc. In Philadelphia's Third District Court, Ginzburg was sentenced to five years in prison by a Judge Body (who referred to him as a "menace to society"). Ironically, while this was going on, the United States Information Service (USIS) had a traveling exhibition overseas which featured *Eros* as an example of the best of American periodicals.

The appeals went through the courts for 10 years. In 1972, the Supreme Court voted 5-4 to uphold the conviction. Ginzburg, absolutely incredulous, planned to chain himself to the pillars of the Jefferson Memorial rather than surrender himself to the U.S. marshals. He was persuaded by his lawyer to forego any dramatization of his plight. "Man, you're out in two weeks. Don't blow it."

Ginzburg acquiesced. He told me it was the worst professional decision of his life. He served eight months of the five-year sentence and paid a fine of $30,000, which wiped him out. Justice Potter Stewart of the Supreme Court said in a speech in Boston a few weeks later that the Court's decision was the worst since Dred Scott. Ginzburg is at present a staff photographer with the *New York Post*.

* * *

H.L. Mencken was asked years after the famous "Hatrack" case (in which, to initiate proceedings against Boston's Watch and Ward Society, he purposely published a story about a Midwestern small-town prostitute who apparently looked like a hatrack and accommodated her customers in a cemetery) whether if he had to do it all over again would he have published "Hatrack." Mencken exclaimed, "Hell, no. . . . My mistake in "Hatrack" was that I didn't follow my own advice. If you're going to fight the moralists, fight them with something that has high literary value in itself, not something you're ashamed of. Fighting for a principle with a piece of inferior goods is sheer foolishness."

This was the problem with the Robert Mapplethorpe photographs, whose showing to the public was the primary cause of the National Endowment's recent difficulties. The specific seven photographs causing all the furor — the so-called *X-Portfolio* — are hardly representative of Mapplethorpe's artistic ability. "Inferior goods." We had a chance to publish them in the *Paris Review*. A lot of headshaking on our part and a quick return of the photos to the Whitney. Indeed, I was astonished that the Corcoran Gallery felt the portfolio even belonged in a Mapplethorpe retrospective.

But this is not the point, of course. It was our editorial decision to return the *X-Portfolio*, not one that was dictated by official restrictions. Across the country restaurants have framed notices announcing in large red letters the occupancy allowances. Quite understandable. But the same kind of restrictive notice, framed and hanging in front of an editor's desk, was not something that we here at the *Paris Review* could condone or even imagine. We felt we had to take some action by returning the NEA grant in protest.

To explain our position, I went down to Washington to testify before a congressional committee. A number of people from the arts were in the hearing room — Roy Lichtenstein, Robert Rauschenberg, Jessica Tandy, Joe Papp (who spoke 20 passionate minutes more than he was allotted, which surprised no one.) and a pianist, a beneficiary of an NEA grant whose rendition of Ravel's "Bolero" practically demolished a stand-up Yamaha piano. The committee chairman was Congressman Sidney Yates from Illinois. At one point a witness apologetically began his testimony by saying that he didn't have much to add . . . that everything had already been said. Yates grinned and interrupted to repeat a remark made years ago in a similar situation by Congressman Smoot (of the Smoot-Harley Tariff Act) that "Yes, everything has been said, but not everybody has said it."

When my turn came to say what had already been said, in part it came out as follows:

"The *Paris Review* gets 20,000 manuscripts a year. We read everything. Some of the stuff is very bad. The worst piece of mail we received this year was a document outlining "General Terms and Conditions For Organizational Grant Recipients" to be agreed to and signed before a grant can be received. Not only as an example of overinflated use of language, but as a guideline, it is truly an insult. One can imagine the distaste with which the document would have been handled (between thumb and forefinger, one can only guess) by such literary magazine editors as Margaret Anderson, James Laughlin, Robert McAlmon, Ford Maddox Ford, Marguerite Caetani, T.S. Eliot, Richard Hugo, Marianne Moore, Philip Rhav, William Phillips, Malcolm Cowley, Edmund Wilson, and others, before being dropped in a wastepaper basket."

I said a few more words and concluded. If I had had more time, I would have mentioned that the perfect relationship between patron and artist (the sort of working arrangement that could exist between the National Endowment and its beneficiaries) was how Tchaikovsky and his patroness from 1877-90, Nadejda von Meck, worked things out. Despite her considerable financial help, there would be no personal relationship between the two; if they happened to meet at concerts it was said they never talked; he acknowledged her presence with a bow. The dedication of an occasional symphony was sufficient.

* * *

Eventually, of course, the National Endowment dropped its insistence on a clause restricting what its recipients wished to do as artists or writers or performers — alas, I have no doubt, because of the pressure of a large number of people actively taking a stand. But it will happen again. The Comstocks are about. The value of a handbook like Dave Marsh's *50 Ways To Fight Censorship* is that advice is provided on how to deal with censors, not only for those directly involved, but for anyone who cares deeply about this important issue — what John Milton referred to as his first freedom: "the liberty to know, to utter, and to argue freely according to conscience . . ."

— GEORGE PLIMPTON
1991

INTRODUCTION

I have a tale to tell
Sometimes it gets so hard to hide it well
I was not ready for the fall
Too blind to see the writing on the wall

— MADONNA, "Live to Tell"

50 Ways to Fight Censorship is a book based on action. It was created to meet a need: the need expressed whenever I wrote an article or made a speech about censorship and people approached me afterwards and said, "But what can we do? " The need that existed throughout the recent war in the Middle East, and that will continue to exist as long as we live in an arms-based economy with an imperially obsessed, covertly theocratic two-party system (in which those two parties often function as one, and never more so than when they are whittling away First Amendment rights).

Often, when people have asked, "But what can we do?" there hasn't been a very good answer. When Salman Rushdie came under a death sentence from a foreign despot, the sophisticated American literary community knew exactly how to respond; it mobilized itself and through a series of pretty simple activities —readings and marches, articles of protest and education — at least momentarily reawakened our countrymen to the danger of suppressing ideas. But when a more everyday crime against the First Amendment is committed by a cop or a senator or a judge or a "community group," even the sophisticates often respond sluggishly. That's especially the case when what's come under attack — a rap record or a comic book, a dirty movie or an extreme political statement — represents culture that's vulgar, simple, tasteless, or dumb, rather than the highbrow, complex, cosmopolitan, and intelligent work of Rushdie. It's all too easy to temporize when what's at stake isn't a "serious novel" or the work of a "fine artist" but the music of a black group specializing in blue humor or the actions of bearded, blue-jeaned revolutionaries.

Over the past seven years of writing and lecturing about censorship in America — primarily about the censorship of popular music — I've learned that there is no way to separate the censorship of one form of expression from that of any other. The attack on Rushdie (which the Reagan-Bush government opposed with great reluctance) is no more separate from the attack on Luther Campbell than the attack on Robert Mapplethorpe is unrelated to Senator Alan Simpson's characterization of CNN reporter Peter Arnett as a "traitor" for reporting what he saw in Baghdad rather than what the generals in Saudi Arabia told him to see. If nothing else, each act of censorship permits the other; once we are acclimated to getting our news from blatantly censored media like radio and TV, we begin to assume, however unconsciously, that what's aberrant is writing or speech that has not been tampered with by the government or some other form of officialdom.

This indivisibility among kinds of censorship is a hard lesson to learn. It wasn't all that easy for me to get it through my own head. I had the great advantage of hearing the words of the ACLU's Barry Lynn echo in my head for a while. Standing outside a Senate hearing room, listening to me spout my doubts about what *some* people thought and said, Lynn mildly observed, "Oh, you only believe in freedom of speech for people you agree with."

It doesn't work that way. (I was going to say, "of course," but in a book like *50 Ways to Fight Censorship*, nothing like that should be taken for granted.) One of the most important lessons of trying to enlist others to fight censorship is that people in the United States no longer know what freedom of speech is, how it works, or what protecting it entails. So take it from me, 'cause I learned the hard way: Cut off one person's voice and you risk having your own larynx removed. No matter how vile you may find what that other guy has to say, there is always a better way to disarm the message than by silencing it.

That's not because words don't hurt. They can be deadly. They can change your life. The point is that the only way to build the kinds of lives that free people ought to have is to allow those words and thoughts to be heard, in all their danger. Get them out in the open, where they can be challenged, endorsed, and, to the extent that they pose social and political riddles, solved. Every other avenue involves deception. And that leads to corruption, and that leads to worse lives for all of us, even for those whose job it is to keep the lid on.

But that's philosophy. The substance of this book is action — an array of things that you can do, and the information about the people and institutions you need to do them with, and do them to. Though the facts are often doleful, the message remains hopeful. These are things that YOU can do — not some special guy with credentials. You. And you. And you. Separately. And most powerfully, together.

Everything needed to start the job of fighting censorship can be found in these pages. I am not certain what it will take to complete the task. Maybe it will never be finished — but then, if you really believe in freedom, eternal vigilance becomes your meat and drink.

— *D.M.*
1991

WHAT IS CENSORSHIP?

In 1984, the American Library Association's Intellectual Freedom Committee adopted the following definitions for terms "frequently used to describe the various levels of incidents which may or may not lead to censorship," which it defined as "the actual removal of materials from open access." None of these conditions is desirable; all infringe upon First Amendment rights of freedom of speech and of the press.

Inquiry — An informational request, usually informal, which seeks to determine the rationale behind the presence of a particular item in a collection.

Expression of Concern — An inquiry that has judgmental overtones. The inquirer has already made a value judgment on the materials in question.

Complaint — A formal written complaint filed with the library, questioning the presence of and/or the appropriateness of specific material.

Attack — A publicly worded statement questioning the value of the material, presented to the media and/or others outside the library organization, in order to gain public support for further action.

Censorship — The removal of material from open access by government authority.

In this book, the word "censorship" is used in its colloquial sense, encompassing all of these definitions.

Ten Commandments for the Fight Against Censorship

1. Emphasize the Positive. The censors do NOT have the right to define the agenda and pick the battleground. Aggressively expose the history of what censorship has done to ruin democracy in countries all over the world. Insist that the greatest peril to our children's education and morals is ignorance and the denial of reality. Remind everyone that unpleasant social realities can't be solved until we all have the right to say openly what's on our minds. Never forget that free speech advocates are parents, good citizens, and (often) good Christians too.

2. You Don't Have to Spend Your Life Living Like a Refugee. The majority of Americans *are* moral; they're also in favor of free speech. A July 1990 *Newsweek* poll showed that 75 percent of Americans felt that the right of adults to "determine what they may see and hear" was "more important" than society having "laws to prohibit material that may be offensive to some segments of the community." So, don't shut up — you don't just have the *privilege* of free speech, you have the *right* to speak, and when that right is threatened, speaking out becomes an *obligation*.

3. On the Other Hand, Remember This: The First Amendment exists to protect speech and activities that are *un*popular. If it only served to protect that which everybody (or "the majority") agreed with, it wouldn't need to be there at all. Limiting free speech is what's *un*American —without it all our other rights and liberties quickly disintegrate. That's why it's the *First* Amendment.

That also means that it's imperative to support independent sources of culture in all the arts, especially given the growing concentration of the publishing, music, and film industries in the hands of a small number of corporate interests. The artists, retailers, and others fighting hardest for free expression tend to be those outside the mainstream of the system. For some art forms — avant garde poetry, the blues, and documentaries, for instance — the independent publishers, record labels, and film distributors provide virtually the only means of existence. So where you have a choice, shop and browse on that basis.

4. *Don't Believe the Hype*. Don't let censors claim they aren't censoring; if it restricts freedom of expression, it's against the First Amendment. One of the most important lessons that censors have learned over the years is never to use the word "censorship." But, as Ali Mazrui wrote in *The Black Scholar*, "Censorship in the U.S. is basically privat-ized . . . freelance censors abound."

Censorship isn't about intentions; it's about consequences. Whether they're presented as "consumer information" or "child protection" or "public safety" (as in the refusal of civic facilities to allow certain kinds of performances to take place), regulations and activities that deny the right to speak ARE forms of censorship, no matter what name their sponsors give them.

5. *Freedom Isn't Free*. The majority of censorship is *economic*, which forces artists to work day jobs to stay alive, and prevents them from creating freely, let alone acquiring the equipment to work with and the space to work in.

Turn some of the ideas in this book into fund-raisers. Use the money you receive to publish and distribute free speech information, to take out anti-censorship ads, to develop and produce free speech public service announcements, and for the legal expenses of those who are censored.

6. *Keep Your Sense of Humor*. This will immediately distinguish you from the censors, who don't have any. Censorship fanatics *never* tell jokes about the issue; they never let the air out of their own bags of wind. Don't be afraid to help them out — or to deflate your own gasbag once in a while.

7. *Remember the Commandment the Censors Forgot:* "Thou shalt not bear false witness against thy neighbors." That doesn't just mean don't lie; it means get the facts straight. So go after those half-truths and expose the lies the censors promote. Make yourself so well-informed that you'll *know* when censors are fabricating facts or distorting "scientific studies," or when they're refusing to acknowledge common sense. If you doubt what they're saying, make 'em *prove* what they're saying is so, and don't let them bluster and bully with anecdotes that never involve names, dates, or places.

8. *Don't Mourn*. Organize seminars and study groups to look at censor-ship in context; accept no easy answers. Find out where attacks on free speech are coming from — even if it means going back 100 or even 500 years. It's important to see both censored and uncensored art. Teach yourself the history of free music, free art, free cinema, etc., so that the lies of the censors won't trick you.

9. *Take Advantage of Resources* — telephones, fax machines, photocopiers — wherever you can find them. It doesn't take an army to make a big difference. Jack Thompson, the Florida censor who launched a campaign that helped get 2 Live Crew indicted, did it all out of his house with a phone and a fax setup. You can fight back effectively using the same kinds of tools.

10. *Contact Other Groups in Your Area* that should have an interest in free speech — not just arts councils, but unions, civil rights organizations, churches, journalists, broadcasters, feminists. Make sure they understand the issue. Ask for their support — and support their causes whenever you can.

50 Ways
to Fight Censorship

1
Speak Out!

Speaking out is the primary duty of every freedom fighter — or good citizen, if you want to put it that way. It's the job that we all have to do, separately and collectively, where we see injustice and where injustice has been going for so long it's become invisible. Silence is a form of censorship, and when important issues are at stake, silence is a form of death.

> THE SINGLE
> MOST
> IMPORTANT
> THING
> YOU CAN DO

• *Talk about censorship.* Don't hide what you feel in order to fit in. Always remember that even if people in so-called "high" culture don't talk much with people in so-called "pop" culture, they face many common enemies. So whether you're a fan or an artist, always be clear about who the enemy is: It's all the people who want to make sure that art and politics have no room for any outlook that's not safe, white, and middle class. By the same token, be clear about who your friends are: They're all the people who make or love art that might displease the powers that be. When you talk to other people about this issue, emphasize what you have in common in the struggle against censorship, then work out your differences.

• *Confront local politicians*, school board and police authorities who practice censorship — speak out at city council meetings and in other public forums. Ask questions, and don't let them waffle on the answers.

• *Attend censorship meetings.* Demand time to speak out with facts that support free speech. You don't have to do this in a way that inhibits the censors' freedom to speak. Point out that just because they may find it unpleasant to hear what they don't want to hear doesn't mean that you're "censoring" them.

• *Sponsor free speech "open mikes,"* events where people can get up and do what they'd like — a poem, a song, a soliloquy. It can be political, nasty, and dangerous. It could be sweet, emotional, and dangerous. Emphasize new voices, particularly those of the disenfranchised, like the homeless. Make it your goal to air new ideas and perspectives, not just the bizarre or shock-oriented: Sometimes these latter things don't bother the censors nearly as much as the pertinent, the real, the true. Stage your open mikes where they're most needed: in bars, cafes, libraries, parks, and for that matter, on rooftops (it won't be the first time art has been made there).

2
Register and Vote!

This is your easiest job — and maybe the most important one.

Registering to vote may seem silly or pointless; you may feel like the system doesn't offer you much choice. But if it helps get the bad guys out of power, and maybe sneaks a few good ones in, it's worth the minimum of effort it requires. After all, and at the risk of sounding like your junior high school civics teacher: *Voting fulfills an essential duty of living in a democracy.*

Freedom of speech and freedom of expression are national concerns with local focus. That means you need to watch for opportunities — just casting a ballot to choose between Tweedledum and Tweedledummer for president every four years won't cut it. Censorship is a matter of education — lots of times, censorship even occurs in schools — so you need to stay up with local school board elections. Censorship is enforced by cops who are either elected (as in the case of county sheriffs) or appointed, and by mayors, city councils, and judges. Anti–free speech bills are introduced at every level, from community councils to state and national legislatures to governors' offices. Later on, you'll read a lot about how to deal with such problems — but NONE of what you learn will have much effect if the same scoundrels keep being re-elected by the same minority of active voters.

Information on voter registration isn't that hard to come by — call the number listed below for your state, and see how fast you can sign up. Then, make sure you get out to the polls on Election Day and actually cast your ballot. Many, if not most, elections are lost because eligible, even registered, voters don't participate. And it's progressive candidates who suffer most from such inaction.

On the other hand, make absolutely certain that you know who you're voting for. Ask candidates to make *specific* commitments on issues about which you're concerned. When a politician endorses the Bill of Rights that doesn't mean he or she opposes censorship. It won't help you much when the guy you vote for insists on labeling records, tossing out textbooks, or hiring porn-crazed prosecutors because "that's not censor-ship, just good government." Don't put yourself in the shoes of the record industry executives who wrote checks to Senator Al Gore. He'd pro-claimed himself an advocate of the arts but then supported his wife when she formed the music censorship group Parents' Music Resource Center, convened a Senate hearing on "porn rock," and generally aided and abetted a national witchhunt targeting rock lyrics. Make the candidate take a stand — before you give a buck, let alone your ballot. After the election, it's too late.

Why Voting in Local Elections Can Be More Important Than Voting in National Elections

Local authorities — councilmembers, mayors, sheriffs, freeholders, judges — are much more likely to effectively censor free speech. They can move much more quickly to ban art, shows, or music than the Congress or the president or the courts. In local communities, a few well-connected censors can have disproportionate power. The primary line of defense against these well-organized free speech opponents is the ballot box.

All of the most striking recent actions against free speech have been local initiatives; the prosecutions involving Robert Mapplethorpe's photo-graphs in Cincinnati and 2 Live Crew's music in Fort Lauderdale are only two of the most notorious examples. Results from juries have shown that the censors are the minority — but elected officials don't feel accountable to the free speech majority, so a few vocal anti-freedom-of-expression fanatics can apply enough pressure to effectively censor a city the size of Cincinnati.

Who Can Vote?

EVERYBODY OVER THE AGE OF 18, who is a United States citizen, can vote. There are very rare exceptions — for instance, convicted felons are disenfranchised. But that's about it.

VOTING IS NOT A PRIVILEGE. IT'S A RIGHT. Beware of phony restrictions. College students should be able to vote in the state where their campus is located *or* at home by absentee ballot. (Obtaining an absentee ballot can be complicated. Check before you leave home.) States sometimes try to disenfranchise those who've recently moved — but if you moved at a time that makes you ineligible to vote in your new town, you should be able to vote in your old one.

Voter Registration Information Lines
(Phone Numbers for Boards of Elections — State by State)

Alabama	(205) 242-7210	Missouri	(314) 751-4875
Alaska	(907) 465-4611	Montana	(406) 444-4732
Arizona	(602) 542-4285	Nebraska	(402) 471-2554
Arkansas	(501) 682-6030	Nevada	(702) 687-3176
California	(916) 445-0820	New Hampshire	(603) 271-3242
Colorado	(303) 894-2211	New Jersey	(609) 292-3760
Connecticut	(203) 566-3106	New Mexico	(505) 827-3621
Delaware	(302) 739-4277	New York	(800) FOR VOTE
District of		North Carolina	(919) 733-2186
Columbia	(202) 727-2525	North Dakota	(701) 224-2905
Florida	(904) 488-7690	Ohio	(614) 466-2585
Georgia	(404) 656-2881	Oklahoma	(405) 521-2391
Hawaii	(808) 453-8683	Oregon	(503) 378-4144
Idaho	(208) 334-2300	Pennsylvania	(717) 787-5280
Illinois	(217) 782-4141	Rhode Island	(401) 277-2345
Indiana	(317) 232-3939	South Carolina	(803) 734-9060
Iowa	(515) 281-5865	South Dakota	(605) 773-3537
Kansas	(913) 296-2236	Tennessee	(615) 741-7956
Kentucky	(502) 564-7100	Texas	(512) 463-5650
Louisiana	(504) 925-7885	Utah	(801) 538-1040
Maine	(207) 289-4186	Vermont	(802) 828-2363
Maryland	(301) 974-3711	Virginia	(804) 786-6551
Massachusetts	(617) 727-2828	Washington	(206) 753-2336
Michigan	(517) 373-2540	West Virginia	(304) 345-4000
Minnesota	(612) 296-2805	Wisconsin	(608) 266-8005
Mississippi	(601) 359-1350	Wyoming	(307) 777-7186

3
Send Your Senators and Congressperson Letters or Mailgrams

Write to your members of Congress. Congressional representatives DO read their mail. And they DO take it seriously. But just to make sure, send a copy of your correspondence to your local newspaper or weekly arts paper. (Journalists also take such letters seriously.)

Congress

Senators are elected from individual states — there are two per state and they represent everybody in the state.

Representatives are elected from districts within each state; they represent all the people in the district, may be as small as a neighborhood (in big cities), or cover an entire state (lightly populated ones have only one representative). Because district lines are haphazard, you may not know who your representative is. Thanks to computer technology, it's now simple to find out. Call the main Capitol telephone number: (202) 224-3121. Tell the operator you want to learn who represents you in Congress. The operator will ask your address and will have the information for you within a few seconds. You can also try the League of Women Voters at (800) 836-6975.

• Write your senators at the Senate Office Building, Washington, DC 20510. Or check your local phone book to see if a district office is listed.

• Write your representative at the House Office Building, Washington, DC 20515; or check your local phone directory for a local office.

Note: Letters sent to Washington are generally more effective than letters sent to local offices. However, there's no reason not to send a copy to each place.

What to Write

Letters should be as personal as possible. Avoid writing a generic or computer-generated letter. These have the least impact — often they aren't even read all the way through — because so many pressure groups use them. In fact, providing you can make it legible, a handwritten letter may make the best impression.

Offer your own views on censorship issues; explain how freedom of speech and how attempts to censor affect you. Tell those in Congress that you will be monitoring their votes on First Amendment issues, and that *you* will vote accordingly. Stick to the subject: Any letter will have more impact if it's written about ONE topic. If you also have environmental concerns, or want to make your point about abortion, write separate letters about those issues.

Be informative as well as emotional. Politicians need to know that you feel strongly about censorship issues. They also need to know the facts; there's so much pro-censorship propaganda floating around those hallowed halls, it won't hurt to set the record straight. DON'T FORGET TO SIGN YOUR NAME AND ADDRESS.

On the other hand, don't overdo it. A few facts are great; an overly detailed harangue may lose sympathy. Make the letter fairly short — a couple of paragraphs, certainly no more than a page to a page-and-a-half will make your case, keep the politician's attention, and help you focus on your main points.

Remember, members of Congress represent you whether or not you voted for them — whether or not you even voted. They ought to be accountable to their constituents, not just their contributors.

Elected officials probably fear you. You're their boss. Take advantage of your political power by *demanding* action to preserve the Bill of Rights.

When to Write

It's especially important to write when major censorship-related issues are presented as new laws or budget matters. For instance, if funding for the National Endowment for the Arts (NEA) is under attack, write in support of the Endowment. Do your best to learn the title of proposed legislation, or the House or Senate bill number it's going under. (Often, these can be gathered from newspaper articles.) Don't expect every member to be familiar with every bill — give them the facts they need to answer you.

Timing can be critical on specific issues. If the newspapers say that a bill is about to "be reported out of committee" or "go to the floor," get your letter or mailgram off ASAP.

But if there's a public issue in your state or town, ask your members of Congress to speak out. If they don't say anything, ask them if they're really in favor of free speech. Also, general inquiries about what they've done to ensure your First Amendment rights can't hurt.

You will definitely get a reply. Often, however, it will be an inappropriate form letter. If you've asked specific questions, and the congressperson has ducked answering them, write back, politely informing your representative that if you do not get a relevant answer, you will have to take the matter up with the press in their home state. If you still don't get an answer, do exactly that.

Flood Their Mailboxes, Haunt Their Hallways

• POSTCARDS are cheap, they'll force you to keep your message short and sweet, and they count as much as letters. If you choose ones with the right image on the other side, they'll send a graphic message, too.

• PRE-PRINTED POSTCARDS are a favorite right-wing tactic that more liberty-lovers ought to use. Print up a basic message on a pre-addressed postcard; all one has to do is sign 'em and mail 'em. The Illinois Coalition Against Censorship used pre-printed postcards to persuade Illinois governor James Thompson to veto a repressive anti-obscenity act passed by the legislature in 1989. The veto held, too.

• MAIL EXHIBITION NOTICES, FLYERS, NEWSLETTERS, maybe even COPIES OF BOOKS, RECORDS, AND VIDEOS to your senators, representatives, governor, state legislators, city councilmembers, mayor, etc. You want these politicians to understand that there are artists, art-lovers, and First Amendment fans living in their district, to know that you're paying attention to them, and to understand that you have just as much claim on their allegiance and attention as the censors. If what you get is a polite form letter acknowledging receipt, consider it the perfect excuse to write back and ask what your representative is doing to protect the First Amendment.

• CONTACT REPRESENTATIVES from elsewhere in your state; state delegations meet regularly and, as a group, they are obliged to respond to constituents. If your congressperson is unsympathetic, find a more friendly one from a neighboring constituency.

Learn the Voting Record of Your Congressperson

These publications can give you an idea of how your senators and representatives vote: *The Congressional Voting Guide* breaks down votes senator-by-senator and congressman-by-congressman, which will give a very good idea of how he or she will vote on key issues. *The Congressional Quarterly Weekly Report* lists congressional votes rollcall-by-rollcall; it's better for tracking specific issues than specific people, but it's more widely available in libraries.

RESOURCES
The Congressional Voting Guide: A Ten Year Compilation of the 100th Congress, by Victor W. Bosnich (self-published, 2nd edition, 1988). Send inquiries to: Victor W. Bosnich, P.O. Box 5385, Dallas, TX 75251; or call (214) 750-5885. The guide costs $27, which includes postage.
The Congressional Quarterly and *The Congressional Quarterly Weekly Report*, found in most good libraries.

4
Teach Your Children How to Know When Censorship Appears in the Classroom, or Elsewhere

• Learn as much as you can about how censorship works and how your child's school and library are affected.

• Write letters to local and national media explaining your opinions on the subject and its effect on kids.

• Show your children the following list of things kids can do to fight

censorship, adapted from Sandra Choron's *The Big Book of Kids' Lists* (New York: Pharos Books, 1985).

Just for Kids

• Talk to your friends about starting a group to fight censorship. Learn about censorship together and talk to other kids, parents, and teachers about how you feel about it. After you've talked with adults, though, make sure you get back together with your friends so you can judge for yourselves whether or not you agree with their ideas and opinions. Make sure what you're told has some *factual* basis — don't take it on faith alone.

• Write to the American Library Association for a list of books that have been banned. (And ask how you can support their annual event, "Banned Books Week.") Some of the books that have been banned will surprise you, because they might be among your favorites: *Are You There God? It's Me, Margaret,* by Judy Blume, as well as many of her other books, because they treat sexual and moral issues realistically; *The Adventures of Sherlock Holmes,* by Sir Arthur Conan Doyle, because it refers to the occult and spiritualism; *Our Bodies, Ourselves,* by the Boston Women's Health Book Collective, because it contains material about how our bodies work; *The Diary of Anne Frank,* by Anne Frank, the diary of a young girl hunted by Nazis during World War II, because it contains allegedly "sexually offensive" material; *To Kill a Mockingbird,* by Harper Lee, about racism in a small Southern town, because it contains the words "damn" and "whore lady"; *Webster's Ninth New Collegiate Dictionary,* for containing "obscene" words (are dictionaries supposed to pretend that people speak a sanitary language?); *The Adventures of Huckleberry Finn,* by Mark Twain, one of the greatest American novels of the 19th century, because one of the characters in this anti-racist saga is named "Nigger Jim." *The Banned Books Week Resource Book* contains a comprehensive list of banned books and is available from the ALA. For ordering information, write the American Library Association's Office for Intellectual Freedom, 50 East Huron Street, Chicago, IL 60611.

• Urge your parents to become involved in fighting for free expression, in your community and elsewhere. Make sure they give you permission to use all library materials, see any film or video, and listen to all forms of music, no matter how much pressure is brought by teachers-turned-cops. Tell them that Bart Simpson's "Underachiever and proud of it" is a slogan that encourages kids to define who they are for themselves.

• Get your friends, family, and other members of your community to sign petitions (see #33) against censorship. Make sure they're delivered to public officials and others who can help. If they won't help, find out why not — and tell others about their failure to honor the First Amendment.

• The Student Press Law Center will help you if school authorities are trying to stop you from writing what you want. Write them at 1755 I Street, NW, Suite 504, Washington, DC 20006; (202) 466-5242.

• Urge your mom and dad to join "Parents for Rock and Rap," founded by retired schoolteacher Mary Morello. PFRR speaks for the majority of music-loving parents and debates censors across the country. Write them at P.O. Box 53, Libertyville, IL 60048.

Censorship Alternatives for Parents

• LISTEN! That means listen to the music that your kids love — it has a lot to tell you about who they think they are, what shape they believe the world's in, the height of their hopes, and the depths of their fears. But it means to *listen to* your kids; just slow down, shut up, and listen to what they have to say. It might be different from what you expect, it might be different from what you want to hear. But it's a message from someone you love. And it's an opportunity to have a conversation you'll remember for the rest of your life. If you really want to help and protect your kids, use your ears before you use your mouth.

• CHOOSE selected censored materials for your children to experience. Help them to select and learn from materials that others want to ban. Explain why *Huckleberry Finn* is a great work of art — and why some people find it offensive. Listen to censored music with them, and discuss its ideas and attitudes, why some people have such feelings and desires, and why others want to repress them. Watch challenged TV shows, like "The Simpsons," together (see #17), and discuss the ideas in them, and why some people want to get rid of these thoughts and concepts. This is the *best* way to educate your children about values and about the issues that make some art controversial.

• FORBID access to materials only with great caution. Do it only after you've heard what your child has to say and only after you've experienced it yourself — don't just take the word of a teacher or a preacher — do it only *after* the most rational discussion you can manage. Try to avoid an outright ban. Explain that some material needs to be scrutinized in relation to existing family values — and that not all families have, or ought to be forced to have — identical values.

• CONTACT musicians, authors, and artists whose work troubles you in regard to your children. Tell them that *your interpretation* of what they're saying is that it's irresponsible. Defend their right to say it, but ask for clarification of purpose. Urge more responsible writing on repugnant issues. SHARE ANY RESPONSE WITH YOUR CHILD.

5
Oppose De Facto Censorship of the News Media by the Wealthy and Powerful

Often, the most subtle and pervasive form of censorship practiced in America comes from media moguls themselves. "There was never any talk of censorship at my paper," said a veteran reporter for a Midwestern daily. "But it was accepted practice that there were things you just didn't report, groups that the owners would forbid you to criticize."

As more and more newspapers, magazines, and radio and TV stations are gobbled up by corporate giants, it's increasingly difficult for reporters, editors, and producers to report some stories "objectively" — or sometimes, to report them at all.

For instance, when Canada's New Democratic Party, a democratic socialist group, won the fall 1990 elections in Ontario, Canada's most populous province, readers of most American newspapers — including the *New York Times* — had to risk severe eye strain to find the news. Those who did cover the story often belittled it, the same way that ABC

"Nightline" 's Ted Koppel did in November 1990, when he interviewed socialist Bernie Sanders, who'd just won Vermont's lone seat in the House of Representatives. (Among other comments, Koppel called Vermont a "wacko" state for electing Sanders.)

It's not just about which stories get covered; it's about who covers them — and with what unspoken biases — that often eliminate certain perspectives from the conversation altogether. We all know how rarely minorities, women, lesbians and gay men, the poor, and the homeless are allowed to speak for themselves on newscasts. But often, even on supposedly "serious" discussion programs, centrists like Jimmy Carter and Bill Bradley are passed off as speaking for "leftists" or "liberals." On CNN's "Crossfire," the "left" is represented by Michael Kinsley, from the right-of-center magazine, the *New Republic*. Meanwhile, such conservatives as Koppel (whose most frequent guest is Vietnam War architect Henry Kissinger), and Diane Sawyer (a former aide to Richard Nixon) are presented as "objective" reporters.

Consequently, we don't know whether "the country has shifted to the right" spontaneously, or as a result of skillful manipulation. We DO know that there are all sorts of sides to the various stories in the news that aren't told. If you have such a tale to tell, the other items in this section may help you find a voice. But even if you don't, you need to seek out as many alternative perspectives as you can, before America and the world sink permanently into war and economic ruin.

• Be aware that if you get your news and opinions solely from major media — the networks and their radio and TV affiliates, daily papers owned by large corporations — you're missing major chunks of reality. Find a good alternative paper and read it; if there's not one where you live, gather your friends and resources and start one. Listen to National Public Radio or Pacifica Radio for alternative perspectives in broadcast news.

• Learn about corporate control of the media. Find out where the power of decision-making rests and how it's influenced by the corporate will. Start by reading Ben Bagdikian's article "The Media Brokers: Concentration and Ownership of the Press," in *Multinational Monitor*, September 1987.

• Support Fairness and Accuracy in Reporting (FAIR), which investigates right-wing news bias on such key topics as labor and national defense. FAIR's newsletter *Extra!* may be the single most important source of current information on this kind of censorship. You can become a member of FAIR for $30 a year; this puts you on the group's "activist list," and gets you a subscription to *Extra!* Contact: FAIR, 130 West 25th Street, New York, NY 10001; (212) 633-6700.

• Call local talk shows and let your voice be heard. If your local station presents only one side of the story, call the station's management and protest.

• Become an *active* member of your public TV or radio station. Just sending a check once a year won't help provide a diversity of perspective. Public radio and TV stations are forever being pushed rightward by management and "economic realities" (i.e., the strictures of corporate sponsorship); that's why such crucial programs as "South Africa Now" and "The Kwitny Report" are dead or dying, while "Firing Line" and other muck proliferates (see # 24).

• Watch for skewed language in "objective" reports on TV, radio, and in the papers. For instance, isn't it curious that management always "offers" while unions always "demand"? That minority leaders are "so-called," while religious crazies are "spokespersons"? That corporate leaders are always allowed to talk their way out of a tight corner — something like Bhopal, say — while activists never are?

• Beware of so-called "watchdogs" like Accuracy in Media and Morality in Media which, under the guise of activism and protest, in fact work to ensure the stability of the status quo.

• Consider boycotting newspapers or radio and TV stations that deny fair access or distort the facts, or, for that matter, the ones that treat their employees unfairly.

• Consult alternative sources of information.

ORGANIZATIONS AND PERIODICALS

Columbia Journalism Review, 700 Journalism Building, Columbia University, New York, NY 10027, (212) 854-2716. To subscribe call (800) 669-1002.

Communications Consortium, 1333 H Street, NW, Suite 1162, Washington, DC 20005, (202) 682-1270

Deadline, Center for War, Peace, and the News Media, New York University, 10 Washington Place, 4th Floor, New York, NY 10003, (212) 998-7960

Essential Information, P.O. Box 19405, Washington, DC 20036, (202) 387-8034

Extra! FAIR (Fairness and Accuracy in Reporting), 130 West 25th Street, New York, NY 10001, (212) 633-6700

Lies of Our Times, Institute for Media Analysis, 145 West 4th Street, New York, NY 10012, (212) 254-1061

Propaganda Review, Media Alliance, Fort Mason Center, Room D-290, San Francisco, CA 94123, (415) 441-2557

BOOKS

The Media Monopoly, by Ben Bagdikian (Boston: Beacon Press, 1983)

Unreliable Sources: A Guide to Detecting Bias in the News Media, by Martin A. Lee and Norman Solomon (New York: Carol Publishing Group, 1990)

Inventing Reality: Politics and the Mass Media, by Michael J. Parenti (New York: St. Martin's Press, 1985)

Radical Media: The Political Experience of Alternative Communication, by John Downing (Boston: South End Press, 1984)

Winning America: Ideas and Leadership for the 1990s, edited by Marcus Raskin and Chester Hartman (Boston: South End Press and the Institute for Policy Studies, 1988)

The Looking-Glass World of Non-Fiction TV, by Elaine Rapping (Boston: South End Press, 1987)

Amusing Ourselves to Death: Public Discourse in the Age of Show Business, by Neil Postman (New York: Penguin, 1986)

Manufacturing Consent: The Political Economy of the Mass Media, by Edward S. Herman and Noam Chomsky (New York: Pantheon, 1988)

A Trumpet to Arms: Alternative Media in America, by David Armstrong (Boston: South End Press, 1984)

6
Get Involved With Your Library

Work with your library's selection committee — by suggesting materials for purchase and by volunteering to support controversial purchases. Stop "market" censorship, in which small town libraries don't purchase controversial books for fear of the reaction. Help fend off censors' protests against current inventory.

The Threat

In 1982, in Calhoun County, Alabama, it started with Doris Day's autobiography. A minister's daughter brought the book home to write a report about it; the minister objected to some of its language. And by the time he and a self-appointed committee of 50 other parents and ministers were done, they'd decided that the county library ought to ban not just Day's book, but Anthony Burgess's *A Clockwork Orange* and everything by John Steinbeck.

It wasn't an isolated incident. During the year ending September 1990, the American Library Association's Office for Intellectual Freedom reported over a thousand attempts to ban books from libraries and schools, including: James Baldwin's *If Beale Street Could Talk*, Larry King's *Tell It to the King* (because it is "an insult to one's intelligence"), Stephen King's *Christine*, Dr. Seuss's *The Lorax* (because it "criminalizes" the forestry industry), and Alice Walker's *The Color Purple*.

No book is safe from the censors. What they fear is an open exchange of ideas. They're worried that once you slip onto the raft with Huck and Jim, or watch Henry Miller banging against the soft walls of the universe, or experience James Baldwin's *Amen Corner*, it may change you.

And *they're right*.

Let's Get It On

You *can* fight back, and Calhoun County offers a good example of how. The librarians themselves led the opposition to censorship. Along with parents, American Civil Liberties Union members, and other concerned citizens, they sent a letter to the supervisor of education and to each member of the board of education, demanding that the book banning stop. They included the American Library Association's Bill of Rights, a 40-year-old document adopted by most public libraries, which states: "[L]ibraries should challenge censorship in the fulfillment of their responsibility to provide information and enlightenment."

Furthermore, Calhoun County's civil libertarians found they could count on national organizations for support. The Authors League of America and International P.E.N. got involved. P.E.N. sponsored a trip to Calhoun by Barbara Beasley Murphy, author of a children's book that had been censored. It proved a lot harder for censors to drum up support for their side when they were confronted with a living, breathing, personable author, clearly not out to send their children's souls directly to hell. And the wave of book banning was turned back.

If your library has a "restricted" shelf — if it limits circulation of certain books, tapes, or videos FOR ANY REASON, if it refuses to acquire by loan or purchase material that you request — ask why.

Your librarian is likely to be your first, best ally.

In Madison, Wisconsin, librarian Don Zermuehlen helped circulate a petition questioning the system over what he and others called "self-censorship." "We're concerned they're turning the library into an agent of the mass media," said Zermuehlen, citing the city library system's refusal to purchase a single $3.50 copy of *Countering the Conspiracy to Destroy Black Boys* by Jawanza Kunjufu while appropriating $1,000 for copies of a biography of Jacqueline Kennedy Onassis.

Here are some things you can do:

• Report all attempts at censorship to your local newspaper.

• Meet with local teachers and other concerned citizens.

• Volunteer to help at your library.

• WRITE OR CALL the following organizations for support, information, and publications:

American Library Association, Office for Intellectual Freedom, 50 East Huron Street, Chicago, IL 60611, (312) 280-4223. The ALA's Office for Intellectual Freedom publishes the bimonthly *Newsletter on Intellectual Freedom*, available for $30 per year, as well as the *Intellectual Freedom Manual* and *Censorship and Selection: Issues and Answers for Schools*.

National Coalition Against Censorship, 2 West 64th Street, New York, NY 10023, (212) 724-1500. NCAC publishes a quarterly newsletter, $25 per year, and also publishes the pamphlets "Books On Trial" and "A Report on Book Censorship and Litigation."

Banned Books Week

Each September, the ALA, the American Booksellers Association, the American Society of Journalists and Authors, the Association of American Publishers, and the National Association of College Stores sponsor "Banned Books Week — Celebrating the Freedom to Read." Designed "to emphasize that imposing information restraints on a free people is far more dangerous than any ideas that may be expressed in that information," the week highlights banned works, encourages citizens to explore new ideas, and provides a variety of materials to promote and display free speech and free press events, including ad slicks, posters, sample press releases, and even a censorship crossword puzzle!

Unfortunately, though the list of participants grows each year, many libraries still don't observe Banned Books Week simply because the demand has not yet been made clear. That's where you come in. Simply call your local library and ask about Banned Books Week. Ask how they plan to participate and how you can help out. The results may surprise you.

But if the librarian seems uncertain, suggest ordering the ALA's pamphlet on the Week. ALA materials are geared toward libraries and librarians (although many booksellers also get involved), but many libraries count on community volunteers for a great deal of their work. This is a great place for you to plug in. So give it a few days, then check back and see what plans are in the works.

Ultimately, if your library isn't interested — and the censorship climate makes many timid — you can turn to your local indepen-dent bookstore. Many such stores, aware that their lives are at stake in the censorship war, already organize at least a Banned Books Week window display.

The American Library Association also publishes the *Newsletter on Intellectual Freedom*, a treasure house of censorship information, as well as a long, annotated list of books and other materials that have been censored.

7
Make Art That Fights Censorship

Make art that fights censorship. For example, make a First Amendment poster to display all over your town — on the sides of buildings, lampposts, the sides of barns, on busy thoroughfares. Use the same ideas, graphics, and slogans to create bumperstickers, T-shirts, and buttons. You can sell these to raise funds for your anti-censorship group.

Try to stay on the right side of the law. It's rarely legal to poster on public utility poles, for reasons stemming from bans on littering and rights of private property. These laws need to be challenged because they discriminate against freedom of the press. Cities allow profit-making newspapers to place their machines on public street corners, and they ought to make space for your civically responsible, unprofitable propaganda. But unless you're willing to fight out the summons in court, be careful about where you stick up your information. (After all, it will have an address or phone number on it, and if the cops want to, they can come after you or your group on this basis.)

• Make an anti-censorship sticker, like the one reading "Book Banning Burns Me Up!" That one's available for 50 cents from H.P. Kopplemann, Inc., Paperback Book Service, P.O. Box 145, Hartford, CT 06141; (800) 243-7724. You can have your own slogan printed up as a sticker or bumpersticker cheaply at many local print shops.

• Order a button, like the bright red one sold by the American Society of Journalists and Authors that reads "I Read Banned Books." Price: $1 for 1-10; less for greater quantities. Write: 1501 Broadway, Suite 1907, New York, NY 10036; (212) 997-0947; FAX: (212) 768-7414. You can get your own buttons and pins made for other censorship issues. Look in the phone book for manufacturers.

• Since graffiti artists are among those most often censored, they might be the perfect artists to involve in your group's efforts. People Like Us, a gay and lesbian bookstore in Chicago, created a Banned Books Week window in graffiti-style spray paint. And of course, you can also buy your own cans of paint and spray slogans in essential spots around town. (Warning: This may violate the law in some places. Find out from your legal adviser!)

• You can create your own T-shirt design, featuring banned records, movies, artists, or a combination of them. (One design that works is the word censorship in a circle, with a red slash drawn across it. But you can be more inventive.) Or come up with a great slogan and emblazon that across your chest. Almost any image that can be photographed can become a T-shirt. T-shirts are printed by lithographers; look them up in your local phone directory and call for prices and other information.

• Write for the National Coalition Against Censorship's pamphlet, "Freedom Is Not a Dirty Word." To celebrate the bicentennial of the First Amendment, the NCAC, which represents 41 national, nonprofit organizations, including religious, educational, artistic, labor, professional, and civil rights groups, created a sort of birthday card. This natty yellow-and-white leaflet graphically displays comments and facts about recent censorship cases. (Unfolded, the interior of the pamphlet is a single statement that can be displayed on bulletin boards or as a poster.) The examples call attention to such issues as pressures against merchants, obscenity challenges in schools, and attacks against films, dictionaries, science, magazines, art, and TV.

NCAC says that "Freedom Is Not a Dirty Word" has been "designed to make three points: (1) offensiveness is not grounds for suppression; (2) the reader's own rights are at stake; and (3) people should feel confident in speaking out when an incident arises — even when, as frequently happens, those demanding suppression seek to frame the issue in a way which denies that censorship is involved."

The pamphlet is available from the Coalition in boxes of 500, for $45 a box, which includes shipping. Write: 2 West 64th Street, New York, NY 10023; (212) 724-1500.

8
Speak Out About Freedom of Speech at Schools, Churches, and to Youth Groups in Your Town

Speaking to local groups can be a great way to raise free speech awareness in your area. Danny Alexander and David Cantwell of Kansas City's rock and anti-censorship newsletter, *A Sign of the Times*, write:

> If you've researched this issue at all then you know more about free speech than the majority of the censors. For that matter, if you're a rock fan, arts connoisseur, avid moviegoer, or even a regular reader, you know more about this issue than anyone who wants to kill art.
>
> Trust that know-how. Half the obstacle in speaking before a group is the fear that you aren't someone worth listening to. You are. One reason you love the arts — especially the kind of arts that come under

censorship attack — is that they've always told you that. In the case of rock and roll, a lot of what it's always been about is people who no one might normally pay attention to getting up on stage with electronically amplified instruments, mikes, and drums. Rock and roll's all about trusting that you've got something important to say — and in different ways, so are all the arts.

Though they may not be wild about the idea, school administrators can hardly refuse to allow speeches and forums dealing with the First Amendment. Approach the student activities office with the idea, emphasizing that current events — record labeling, 2 Live Crew and the Mapplethorpe headlines, the advent of NC-17 ratings, the banning of Salman Rushdie's book *The Satanic Verses*, Cable News Network's fight over the Noriega tapes — makes a free speech talk a popular event, one that will at the same time challenge students to think critically about issues as academically traditional as political science. The same strategy can be applied to youth groups, who, though ostensibly formed by and for youth, are often conservative and adult-dominated in their decision-making process.

Churches are also very important places to speak out on First Amendment issues. Our country's foundation on religious freedoms may have been directly tied to the rights of people to say what they wanted to say, and worship what they wanted to worship, but some churches seem to be among the first places to overlook the need for free speech. Too often, in place of a sermon, guest speakers wax on about the evils of heavy metal and rap music, all the while further alienating the young people they hope to influence. When this sort of thing happens, demand the opportunity to challenge the speaker's authority — if not by asking questions on the spot then (maybe even better) in a talk the following week. If your church respects you as a member, it must allow your side of the story to be told. Gather church literature. If other churches in your area sponsor pro-censorship speeches or meetings, ask that you might be allowed to offer another perspective on the subject.

Whatever you do, don't allow free speech issues to go unnoticed in your town. Too often, forums on these issues feature "experts" who neither like rock and roll and other arts nor see the urgency of problems like record labeling and the denial of grants. At a recent anti-censorship forum at one of our area high schools, the most intelligent comments consistently came from the students asking questions — not the panel of disc jockeys and record retailers who tended to treat our art as merely a product to be bought and sold. Rock fans, like other art lovers, know it is also much more. That's why their voices — your voices — must be heard.

RESOURCES

A Sign of the Times, P.O. Box 2363, Shawnee Mission, KS 66201. Kansas City's

rock and anti-censorship newsletter, $5 for a one-year subscription.
The Center for Civic Education, 5146 North Douglas Fir Road, Calabasas, CA 91302; (818) 340-9320. Develops curriculum materials to teach high school students about the Constitution.

9
Write a Letter to Your Local Paper in Defense of Free Speech

Writing a letter to the editor of your local paper can be very effective. This can be a general letter in defense of free speech or, maybe more important, it can be a letter responding to an irresponsible article on "shock rock," "violent films," "sacrilegious art," or library censorship. Demand a story airing the truth, or at least one reflecting other points of view. Complain about the laziness of reporters who allow themselves to be spoon-fed by censors like the Parents' Music Resource Center and Focus on the Family.

Censorship is a hot topic and letters to the editor in the local press are avidly read by many people, including those who never hear about the on-going debate that takes place only in the national media. You can usually find the address and phone number of the paper in a box on the editorial page — or just look in the phone book. Read some copies of the paper before sending your letter — that way you'll have an idea of the kind of length, style, and so on that's likely to be published.

A good letter to the editor may also be used as a petition (see #33), whether or not the paper prints it. In fact, you can send the letter with a group of signatures and then circulate it around town as a petition. Or, if your paper doesn't want to print such a letter, you can circulate a petition demanding that the paper print free speech points of view.

You should also find out why your local paper covers the censorship issue, or why it doesn't. Ask why the paper covers certain issues, but leaves other important ones on the cutting room floor. Much, if not most, censorship takes place by omission: For instance, a labor leader like

Poland's Lech Walesa is reverently covered but domestic trade unionists are virtually never asked for their perspective on U.S. issues. Many key American strikes and other labor disputes (notably the Pittston coal field battles of 1989-90) are barely covered at all. Stories about national health insurance quote private insurance industry sources and the conservative M.D.s at the American Medical Association, but no advocates of socialized medicine or alternative health practitioners. A Washington-financed dictator like Saddam Hussein becomes a "Hitler" when he refuses to do the U.S. government's bidding, but his butchery is covered as a mere "excess" when he's cooperating with U.S. interests. Because we believe most of what we read, and because that which isn't covered presumably doesn't exist, the public can easily be misled by lazy or biased journalism. Politely, but firmly, demand that your paper tell you what's really going on in society.

You can generate local press coverage by going with an organized group to the city council and demanding an ordinance protecting free speech on "obscenity" issues. Help yourself by always timing events to meet media deadlines, and by learning which reporters (not only at the newspapers, but also at TV and radio stations) are sympathetic. Or at least know which ones are going to *do* the stories, so you can work with them — or around their prejudices.

10
Call Your Radio Station Talk Show

James Bernard, West Coast editor of *The Source* (the "bible of hip-hop"), writes:

> Talk radio is a low profile, but powerful, cultural force in America, so call in. Talk radio shows are daily town meetings, a place for us to engage our neighbors on a wide variety of topics. There are over 200 talk radio programs across the country, and all of them hook right into our communities, speaking directly with people in their homes, workplaces, and cars. Unlike television talk shows, this is a two-way communi-

cation; all it takes is a phone call, and you're on the air. Talk radio hosts, as well as their audiences, defy easy stereotypes, ranging from tabloid-style, self-proclaimed screaming "loudmouths" to generalists like Larry King.

Talk radio can be a very effective forum through which to fight censorship. In recent memory, talk radio hosts have flexed their political muscle with impressive results. For example, in 1986, Jerry Williams of WRKO-AM in Boston used his radio show to collect 40,000 signatures in a petition drive that resulted in the repeal of the state's mandatory seat belt law. On a national scale, Ralph Nader's calls to talk show hosts helped spark the backlash against the proposed congressional pay raise in 1989.

You should use these shows as a way to tell your neighbors and friends why you hate censorship and what *they* can do about censorship. There is no blueprint "how-to" for approaching these shows, but there are some tips:

• KNOW YOUR HOST: Since talk shows are all very different — with varying political bents, temperaments, and "pet" subjects — it's a good idea for you to listen to a show before you call. You want to figure out which buttons to push so you can get the host on your side. For example, if the host is a libertarian-type, you can catch his or her ear by couching your argument in keep-the-government-out-of-our-lives rhetoric. If the host is more of a populist, you may want to make it clear that you're on the "side of the little guy." Also, you'll want to check out how they treat callers. Some will let you talk without interruption while others will begin firing questions as soon as they get you on the line.

• DON'T READ: Very few talk show hosts will be patient with a caller who appears to be reading a statement. This is not to say that you should not prepare. Make notes and think through your argument, but do not read. You may even want to have a friend ask you questions beforehand, to make sure that you can make yourself clear on the air.

• BE SPECIFIC: In addition to educating the audience, you also want to get them or the host to *do* something to fight censorship. It's best to talk about a specific incident — an artist or TV show targeted by censors, or a band whose music is being taken out of the record stores — rather than in generalities like "censorship is bad." Also, it is important to suggest a course of action: For example, "I'm going to write a letter to protest what they did and all of your listeners should, too." Give names and addresses or phone numbers so people know to whom they should address their protest, or their support — whether it's financial or moral support. If you're lucky, you will convince the host to take up the anti-censorship banner after you've hung up. Radio hosts are concerned with ratings and popularity just like their television counterparts, so if your call generates other similar calls, he or she will not want to miss out on such a "hot" issue.

11
Support Those Retailers Who Fight Against Censorship

Boycott retailers who surrender to censorship. Shopkeepers who don't stand up to censors don't deserve your business. Those who do deserve all the support you can give them.

Ask Retailers to Spread the Word

Many people who own or manage record shops, bookstores, or video stores strongly support the arts through which they make a living. Ask them to show that support by letting their stores serve as clearinghouses for information on censorship battles.

Then help them set up a display of books, records, or videos that censors have targeted. Hang a map of the United States, highlighting cities where censors have restricted access to books, records, or films. Create a community bulletin board on which to post reports on censorship activities and publicize anti-censorship activities. Display the names, addresses, and phone numbers of your local elected officials, and those of local and national groups fighting for free expression.

Write Your Local Retailer

If a record store, bookstore, or video outlet will not sell certain albums, books, or movies, send a letter of protest to the store's manager, and ask for an explanation. Do the same if the shop imposes limits on who can buy certain titles. But don't stop there.

If the store is part of a larger chain, as many are, send a copy of your letter to the company headquarters. Send another copy to local newspapers, news radio (and/or music radio) stations, asking them to look into the retailer's actions.

MAJOR MUSIC RETAIL CHAINS

(Note: Not all of these chains do business under their corporate name; we've listed many store names in parentheses, so check carefully to see if your local store is part of a chain.)

Almor Playtime (Record Giant), P.O. Box 270, Amsterdam, NY 12010, (518) 843-3801

Believe in Music, 2300 Oak Industrial Drive NE, Grand Rapids, MI 49505, (616) 534-5755

Best Buy, 4400 West 78th Street, Bloomington, MN 55435, (612) 896-2300

Buzz Enterprises (Buzzard's Nest), 333 Highfield Drive, Columbus, OH 43214, (614) 888-6698

Camelot Enterprises, Inc. (Fisher Big Wheel, Spectrum Audio-Video), 8000 Freedom Avenue NW, North Canton, OH 44770, (216) 494-2282

Cavages (Crazy Charlie), 2600 Walden Avenue, Buffalo, NY 14225, (716) 685-2400

Central South Music Sales (Music 4 Less, Sound Shop), 3730 Vulcan Drive, Nashville, TN 37211, (615) 833-5960

CML Inc. (Music Vision), 660 Harding Avenue, Maryland Heights, MO 63043, (314) 291-0608

Entertainment Enterprises (Boogie Records, Karma Records), 403 Industrial Drive, Carmel, IN 46032, (317) 844-6271

Flip Side, 647 South Vermont Street, Palatine, IL 60067, (708) 202-1000

Harmony House, 1755 East Maple Road, Troy, MI 48083, (313) 524-2800

Kemp Mill, 11420 Old Baltimore Pike, Beltsville, MD 20705, (301) 595-9880

Lechmere, 275 Wildwood Street, Woburn, MA 01801, (617) 935-8320

Mainstream Records, 8201 West Silver Spring Drive, Milwaukee, WI 53218, (414) 438-4400

MTS Inc. (Tower Records/Tower Video), P.O. Box 919001, West Sacramento, CA 95691, (916) 373-2500

Music City Record Distribution (Cat's), 25 Lincoln Street, Nashville, TN 37210, (615) 255-7315

Music Promotions, Inc. (Record and Tape Outlet), 6740 Huntley Road, Suite J, Columbus, OH 43229, (614) 785-9600

Musicland Group (Discount Records, Sam Goody, JC Penney), 7500 Excelsior Boulevard, Minneapolis, MN 55426, (612) 932-7700

National Record Mart (NRM Music, Oasis, Waves), 5607 Baum Boulevard, Pittsburgh, PA 15206, (412) 441-4100

One-Stop Record House, Inc. (Peppermint Records and Tapes), 881 Memorial Drive SE, Atlanta, GA 30316, (404) 223-0144

Pacific Coast One-Stop (Nickelodeon, Tempo), 9158 Eton Avenue, Chatsworth, CA 91311, (818) 709-3640

Peaches, 3451 Executive Way, Miramar, FL 33025, (305) 432-4200

Pegasus, 901 East Highway 193, Layton, UT 84040, (801) 771-4053

Radio Doctors, 240 West Wells Street, Milwaukee, WI 53203, (414) 276-6422

Rainbow Records, 29987 Ahearn Avenue, Union City, CA 94587, (415) 487-6300

Record Bar (Tracks), 3333 Chapel Hill Boulevard, Durham, NC 27707, (919) 493-4511

Record Den (Music Box), 1774 East 40th Street, Cleveland, OH 44103, (216) 391-6464

Record Shop, 2330 Marinship Way, Suite 207, Sausalito, CA 94965, (415) 331-7464

Record Theater, 1800 Main Street, Buffalo, NY 14208, (716) 881-0654

Record World (Square Circle), 22 Harbor Park Drive, Port Washington, NY 11576, (516) 621-2500

Show, Industries (Music Plus), P.O. Box 58900, Los Angeles, CA 90058, (213) 234-3336

Sight and Sound Distributors (Penny Lane Records, Streetside Records), 2055 Walton Road, St. Louis, MO 63114, (314) 426-2388

Sound Warehouse, 10911 Petal Street, Dallas, TX 75238, (214) 343-4700

Spec's Music, 1666 NW 82nd Avenue, Miami, FL 33126, (305) 592-7288

Starship Music, Inc., 6753 Jonesmill Court, Suite B, Norcross, GA 30092, (404) 448-9520

Sterling Ventures, Inc. (Rose Records), 3010 North Oakley, Chicago, IL 60618, (312) 281-8444

Strawberries (Waxie Maxie's), 205 Fortune Boulevard, Milford, MA 01757, (508) 478-2031

Target Stores, 33 South Sixth Street, Minneapolis, MN 55440, (612) 370-6073

Third World Enterprises, 486 Decatur Street, Atlanta, GA 30312, (404) 688-5958

Trans World Music Group (Coconuts, Good Vibrations, Great American Music, The Music Co., Record Town, Tape World), 38 Corporate Circle, Albany, NY 12203, (518) 452-1242

Turtle's, 2151 Northwest Parkway, Marietta, GA 30067, (404) 988-9805

Variety Co., 912 Professional Place, Suite E, Chesapeake, VA 23320, (804) 547-1297

Wall to Wall (Beaky's, Bravo, Listening Booth), 200 South Route 130, Cinnaminson, NJ 08077, (609) 786-8300

Waxworks (Disc Jockey Records, Music Express), 325 East Third Street, Owensboro, KY 42301, (502) 926-0008

Wee Three Record Shops, 3900 Main Street, Philadelphia, PA 19127, (215) 676-1250

Western Merchandisers (Hastings), P.O. Box 32270, Amarillo, TX 79120, (806) 353-4755

Wherehouse Entertainment (Leopold, Odyssey), 19701 Hamilton Avenue, Torrance, CA 90502, (213) 538-2314

The Wiz, 58-30 Grand Avenue, Maspeth, NY 11378, (718) 886-5500

SOME MAJOR BOOKSTORE CHAINS

B Dalton Bookseller (a division of Barnes & Noble), 122 Fifth Avenue, New York, NY 10011, (212) 633-3300

Barnes & Noble Bookstores, Inc., 122 Fifth Avenue, New York, NY 10011, (212) 633-3300

Bookland Inc., 1135 South Edgar Street, York, PA 17403, (717) 843-0279

Brentano's (a division of Waldenbooks), 201 High Ridge Road, Stamford, CT 06904, (203) 352-2000

Crown Books, 3300 75th Avenue, Landover, MD 20785, (301) 731-1200

Doubleday Book Shops, 245 Park Avenue, 43rd Floor, New York, NY 10167, (212) 984-7052

Encore, 424 Railroad Avenue, Shermanstown, PA, (717) 731-4702

Follett College Stores, P.O. Box 888, Elmhurst, IL 60126, (708) 279-2330

Hastings Books & Records, 15 Western Plaza, Suite 17, Amarillo, TX 79106, (806) 355-8471

Krock's & Brentano's, Inc., General Office and Main Store, 29 South Wabash Avenue, Chicago, IL 60603, (312) 332-7500

Lauriat's, Inc., 10 Pequot Way, Canton, MA 02021, (617) 828-8300

Little Professor Book Centers Inc., 110 North Fourth Avenue, Ann Arbor, MI 48104, (313) 994-1212

Waldenbooks, Inc., 201 High Ridge Road, Stamford, CT 06904, (203) 352-2000

Zondervan Family Bookstores, Corporate Office, 1415 Lake Drive SE, Grand Rapids, MI 49506, (616) 698-6900

VIDEO RETAILERS

Blockbuster Video (owners of Applause, Major, and other smaller chains), 901 East Las Olas Boulevard, Fort Lauderdale, FL 33301, (305) 524-8200

Movieland, USA, 4120 Rogers Avenue, Fort Smith, AR 72901, (501) 783-4737

National Video, 9990 Global Road, Philadelphia, PA 19115, (800) 433-5171
Top Hat Video, 902 East 900 South, Salt Lake City, UT 84105, (801) 355-1104
Video Biz, 2981 West State Road 434, Suite 100, Longwood, FL 32779,
(800) 582-7347
Video Galaxy, 101 West Street, Rockville, CT 06066, (203) 871-7831
West Coast Video, 990 Global Road, Philadelphia, PA 19115, (215) 677-1000

12
Read Everything You Can Get Your Hands On About Censorship and First Amendment Issues; Read Banned Books

Read everything you can about censorship and First Amendment issues. Your reading list should include banned books and magazines —not just books *about* free expression. You should even, in the spirit of "know your enemy," read material written by censors.

You should definitely read as many of the following publications as possible. Not only will they you make much better informed and more effective as an anti-censorship activist, but just as important, you'll feel much less isolated in your pro–First Amendment attitudes.

RESOURCES

The Coalition of Writers Organizations (COWO) regularly issues large packets of clippings on pro- and anti-censorship news from around the country. Send $20 to Associated Writing Programs, Old Dominion University, Norfolk, VA 23508.

The *Newsletter on Intellectual Freedom*, 50 East Huron Street, Chicago, IL 60611, (312) 944-6780, is a bimonthly publication of the American Library Association that reports censorship incidents across the U.S., summarizes recent First Amendment court cases, and offers a bibliography. (Subscription: $30 per year.)

The *Gauntlet*, 309 Powell Road, Springfield, PA 19064, discusses general censorship issues in a highly readable fashion, often written by "name" writers and other public figures. This is perhaps the only publication that takes attacks on high culture and pop culture equally seriously.

Rock & Roll Confidential is a monthly newsletter edited by Dave Marsh. RRC is the single best source of information on music censorship because its "You've Got A Right To Rock" campaign reaches into every state and sometimes across international borders. For a one-year subscription, send $19.95 to RRC, P.O. Box 341305, Los Angeles, CA 90034.

The Source is the best rap music magazine in the U.S. and its coverage of rap censorship makes essential reading. For a one-year subscription send $19.95 to *The Source*, 594 Broadway, New York, NY 10012; (212) 274-0464.

Jello Biafra's No More Censorship Defense Fund, P.O. Box 11458, San Francisco, CA 94101, raises money to defend those charged in censorship cases. Other activities include a newsletter, an archive of censorship information, and petition drives.

Z-PAC, Frank Zappa's political lobbying arm, will send you a packet of information on music censorship. Send $1.50 and a stamped, legal-size, self-addressed envelope to P.O. Box 5265, North Hollywood, CA 91616, or call (818) 764-0777. (Pick up on Zappa's *The Real Frank Zappa Book* for a sometimes side-splitting, always illuminating, account of Frank's career-long brushes with blue-noses.)

The Freedom Writer, published by the Institute for First Amendment Studies, is "the national newsletter that defends the separation of church and state." It deals with a whole other aspect of the First Amendment and basically sees itself as a watchdog against theocracy. But it frequently offers important insights and information about church leaders who also practice or encourage censorship (its coverage of Rev. Donald Wildmon is particularly thorough), and often includes generic censorship facts. There is no subscription fee; the newsletter is sent to members — dues are $25 a year. Write them at: P.O. Box 589, Great Barrington, MA 01230; (413) 274-3786.

The U.S. Constitution Bicentennial: A We The People Resource Book, by Robert P. Doyle and Susan A. Burk and *The Bicentennial of the Bill of Rights: A Resource Book* are designed to assist local organizers in getting attention to Constitutional values. They're $10 each, from ALA Graphics, Public Information Office, 50 East Huron Street, Chicago, IL 60611; (312) 944-6780.

Liberty Denied: The Current Rise of Censorship in America, by Donna Demac, with a preface by Arthur Miller, shows the extent of the assault on free expression, especially the way this assault has imposed hidden limits on political debate about domestic and foreign policy issues. It's $6.95 plus tax, from PEN American Center, 568 Broadway, New York, NY 10012; (212) 334-1660.

Bookbanning in America: Who Bans Books and Why by William Noble, $21.95 (Middlebury, VT: Eriksson, 1990), offers a concise, fact-crammed history of American print censorship.

The following writers' organizations can also be contacted for information:

The Authors League of America, 234 West 44th Street, New York, NY 10036, (212) 391-9198

PEN American Center, 568 Broadway, New York, NY 10012, (212) 334-1660. PEN American Center publishes a quarterly newsletter; $5 per year.

PEN Center U.S.A. West, 1100 Glendon Avenue, Suite 850, Los Angeles, CA 90024, (213) 824-2041. PEN West publishes a quarterly newsletter, $5 per year.

50 Great Banned* Books

(The following list is excerpted from *Banned Books Week '90: Celebrating the Freedom to Read*, published by the American Library Association.)

1. **Address to the German Nobility** — Martin Luther. Prohibited by edicts of the Emperor and the Pope (1521).

2. **The Adventures of Sherlock Holmes** — Sir Arthur Conan Doyle. Banned in the USSR (1929) because of its references to occultism and spiritualism.

3. **The Age of Reason** — Thomas Paine. Author and publisher both imprisoned in England.

4. **Alice's Adventures in Wonderland** — Lewis Carroll. Suspended from classroom use, pending review, at the Woodsville High School in Haverhill, NH (1900), because the novel contains expletives, references to masturbation and sexual fantasies, and derogatory characterizations of a teacher and of religious ceremonies.

5. **American Heritage Dictionary**. Removed from school libraries in Anchorage, AK (1976); Cedar Lake, IN (1976); Eldon, MO (1977); and Folsom, CA (1982) due to "objectionable" language.

6. **As I Lay Dying** — William Faulkner. Challenged as a required reading assignment in advanced English class of Pulaski High School in Somerset, KY (1987), because the book contains "profanity and a segment about masturbation."

7. **The Bell Jar** — Sylvia Plath. Prohibited for use in the Warsaw, IN, schools (1979). Challenged in Edwardsville, IL (1981).

---

*The word "banned" is used here, and throughout this book, in a liberal sense, to imply that a book (or record or work of art) was challenged, censored, and/or made unavailable to the public in a particular library, school district, state, etc. at a particular time — and not nesessarily that all people were legally forbidden to read it (or listen to it or look at it).

8. **The Best Short Stories by Negro Writers** — Langston Hughes, ed. Removed from the Island Trees, NY Union Free District High School library in 1976, along with nine other titles, because they were considered "immoral, anti-American, anti-Christian, or just plain filthy"; returned to the library after the U.S. Supreme Court ruling on June 25, 1982 in *Board of Education, Island Trees Union Free School District No. 26, et al v. Icao, et al.*

9. **Biology** — Karen Arms and Pamela S. Camp. Garland, TX Independent School District's central textbook selection committee (1985) withdrew its recommendation because the text includes "overly explicit diagrams of sexual organs, intricate discussion of sexual stimulation, and the implication of abortion as a means of birth control."

10. **Brave New World** — Aldous Huxley. Banned on grounds of obscenity in Boston, MA (1930). A Baltimore, MD (1952) schoolteacher was dismissed for assigning Huxley's novel to a senior literature class. The teacher's unsuccessful quest for vindication is reported in *Parker v. Board of Education*, 237 F. Supp. (D. Md.).

11. **Candide** — François Voltaire. Seized by U.S. Customs in Boston, MA (1929) and declared obscene; suppressed in the USSR (1935). Voltaire's best-known work remained anathema to American authorities as late as 1944, when Concord Books issued a sale catalog that included the book and was informed by the U.S. Postal Service that such a listing violated U.S. postal regulations against sending obscene matter through the mails.

12. **Catch-22** —Joseph Heller. Challenged at the Dallas, TX Independent School District high school libraries (1974), and in Snoqualmie, WA (1979) because of several references to women as "whores."

13. **The Catcher in the Rye** — J.D. Salinger. Banned from classrooms in Boron, CA high school (1989) because the book contains profanity.

14. **Charlie and the Chocolate Factory** — Roald Dahl. Removed from a locked reference collection at the Boulder, CO Public Library (1988). The book was originally locked away because the librarian thought the book espoused a poor philosophy of life.

15. **A Clockwork Orange** — Anthony Burgess. Removed from high school classrooms in Westport, MA (1977) and Aurora, CO (1976) due to "objectionable" language; removed from two Anniston, AL high school libraries (1982), but later reinstated on a restricted basis.

16. **Daddy Was a Number Runner** — Louise Meriwether. Removed from all Oakland, CA junior high school libraries (1977) and its use restricted in senior high schools, following a complaint about the book's explicit depiction of ghetto life.

17. **Declaration of Independence** — Vladimir I. Lenin. Banned in Oklahoma City, OK (1940). Bookstore owners were sentenced to 10 years in prison and fined

$5,000 for selling Lenin's work.

18. Dialogue Concerning the Two Chief World Systems — Galileo Galilei. Banned by Pope Urban VIII for heresy and breach of good faith (1633).

19. Diary of Anne Frank — Anne Frank. Challenged in Wise County, VA (1982) due to protests by several parents who complained that the book contains sexually offensive passages. Four members of the Alabama State Textbook Committee (1983) called for the rejection of this title because it is a "real downer."

20. The Divine Comedy — Dante Alighieri. Burned in Florence, Italy (1497). Prohibited by church authorities in 1581 in Lisbon, Portugal, until all copies were delivered to the Inquisition for correction.

21. Faust — Johann Wolfgang von Goethe. Production suppressed in Berlin (1908) until certain dangerous passages concerning freedom were deleted. Franco purged Spanish libraries of all of Goethe's writings (1939).

22. Garfield: His Nine Lives — Jim Davis. Moved to adult section of the public libraries of Saginaw, MI (1989) after patrons requested that children be denied access.

23. Go Ask Alice — Anonymous. The Gainesville, GA Public Library (1986) prohibits young readers from checking out this anti-drug novel. Forty other books, on subjects ranging from hypnosis to drug abuse to breast-feeding to sexual dysfunction, are also kept in a locked room.

24. The Great Gatsby — F. Scott Fitzgerald. Challenged at the Baptist College in Charlestown, SC (1987) because of "language and sexual references in the book."

25. Guide of the Perplexed — Maimonides. Barred from Jewish homes, and anyone reading it was excommunicated; the work was still facing bans in the 19th century. Maimonides was probably the first Jewish author to have his works burned.

26. The Happy Prince and Other Stories — Oscar Wilde. Challenged at the Springfield, OR Public Library (1988) because the stories were "distressing and morbid."

27. Howl and Other Poems — Allen Ginsberg. In 1956, the year the book was published, Lawrence Ferlinghetti was arrested in San Francisco for selling the book and Ginsberg was brought up on obscenity charges.

28. If Beale Street Could Talk — James Baldwin. Removed from the St. Paul, OR High School library (1989) because the book contains obscene language and explicit descriptions of sexual activity.

29. Invisible Man — Ralph Ellison. Excerpts banned in Butler, PA (1975); removed from the high school English class reading list in St. Francis, WI (1975).

30. J'accuse — Emile Zola. Listed on the Index Librorum Prohibitorum in Rome (1898); banned in Yugoslavia (1929); and in Ireland (1953).

31. **Lady Chatterley's Lover** — D.H. Lawrence. Banned by U.S. Customs (1929).

32. **The Last Temptation of Christ** — Nikos Kazantzakis. Challenged in Long Beach, CA (1962-65).

33. **Leaves of Grass** — Walt Whitman. The district attorney in Boston, MA (1881) threatened political prosecution unless the volume was expurgated.

34. **Madame Bovary** — Gustave Flaubert. Placed on the Index Librorum Prohibitorum in Rome (1864). Banned by the National Organization of Decent Literature (1954).

35. **Mein Kampf** — Adolf Hitler. Banned in Palestine (1937) and in Czechoslovakia (1932).

36. **Mother Goose: Old Nursery Rhymes** — Arthur Rackman, illus. Challenged at the Dade County, FL Public Library (1983) by a Miami metro commissioner because the anthology contains the following anti-Semitic verse: "Jack sold his gold egg / to a rogue of a Jew / who cheated him out of / half of his due."

37. **Naked Lunch** — William Burroughs. Found obscene by Boston, MA Superior Court (1965). The finding was reversed by the state's supreme court the following year.

38. **1984** — George Orwell. Challenged in Jackson County, FL (1984) for being "pro-communist" and containing "explicit sexual matter."

39. **The Odyssey** — Homer. Plato suggested expurgating Homer for immature readers (387 B.C.) and Caligula tried to suppress it because it expressed ideals of freedom.

40. **Oliver Twist** — Charles Dickens. A group of Jewish parents in Brooklyn, NY (1949) went to court claiming that the assignment of Dickens's novel, which features the stereotyped Jewish criminal mastermind Fagin, to senior high school literature classes violated the rights of their children to receive an education free of religious bias (*Rosenburg v. Board of Education of the City of New York*).

41. **On the Origin of Species** — Charles R. Darwin. Banned from Trinity College in Cambridge, England (1859). Banned in Yugoslavia (1935), and in Greece (1937). The teaching of evolution was prohibited in Tennessee from 1925-67.

42. **One Hundred Years of Solitude** — Gabriel García Márquez. Purged from the book list used at the Wasco, CA Union High School (1986) because the book, by the winner of the 1982 Nobel Prize for literature, was "garbage being passed off as literature."

43. **Our Bodies, Ourselves** — Boston Women's Health Book Collective. Challenged at the William Chrisman High School in Independence, MO (1984) because the book is "filthy." The controversial feminist health manual was on a bookshelf in a classroom and was the personal property of the teacher.

44. **The Rolling Stone Illustrated History of Rock and Roll 1950-1980** — Jim

Miller, ed. Challenged in Jefferson County, KY (1982) because it "will cause our children to become immoral and indecent."

45. The Satanic Verses — Salman Rushdie. Banned in Pakistan, Saudi Arabia, Egypt, Somolia, the Sudan, Malaysia, Qatar, Indonesia, South Africa, and India because of its criticism of Islam. Burned in West Yorkshire, England (1989) and temporarily withdrawn from two bookstore chains in the U.S. on the advice of police who took threats against the stores seriously.

46. The Shining — Stephen King. Removed from the Evergreen School District's four junior high school libraries in Vancouver, WA (1986) because the book's "descriptive foul language made it unsuitable for teenagers."

47. Slugs — David Greenberg. Banned from the Escondido, CA Elementary School District libraries (1985) because its graphic depiction of "slugs being dissected with scissors" and its verses describing the roasting, toasting, stewing, and chewing of the creatures were "unsuitable and should not have been allowed in the libraries in the first place."

48. To Kill a Mockingbird — Harper Lee. Challenged in Eden Valley, MN (1977) and temporarily banned due to the words "damn" and "whore lady" used in the novel.

49. Tropic of Cancer — Henry Miller. Banned by U.S. Customs (1934). The U.S. Supreme Court found the novel not obscene (1964).

50. Ulysses — James Joyce. Burned in U.S. (1918), in Ireland (1922), in Canada (1922), and in England (1923), and banned in England (1929).

13
Gather Information and News Clippings on Censorship and Send Them to a Central Clearinghouse

Censorship information needs to be summarized and distributed nationally, in order to increase awareness and activity. Most people in America, even those concerned with censorship, aren't aware of what's happening outside their own city or immediate area of interest. By sharing information, people become more aware of how dangerous the threat is and become more active in combating it.

Send clippings to national connecting points. Here's a partial list:

MUSIC IN GENERAL: *Rock & Roll Confidential*, P.O. Box 341305, Los Angeles, CA 90034.

RAP MUSIC: GRIP (Group for Rap Industry Protection), P.O. Box 4856, Berkeley, CA 94704.

GRAFFITI ART: Can Control, P.O. Box 406, North Hollywood, CA 91603.

LITERATURE: Office for Intellectual Freedom, c/o American Library Association, 50 East Huron Street, Chicago, IL 60611.

ARTS FUNDING: Center for Arts Advocacy, c/o Arts Partners, 861 West Wrightwood, Chicago, IL 60614.

GENERAL: *The Gauntlet*, 309 Powell Road, Springfield, PA 19064.

14
Buy Banned Records; Fight Record Labeling

Support banned music. Buy banned records and request banned songs at concerts and on the radio.

Why Record Labeling Is Censorship

We've adapted the three key reasons why record labeling is censorship, offered by the No More Censorship Defense Fund in its "Fact Sheet #4":

1. Major music distributors have made it clear that they will not carry albums that bear warning stickers. Musicians who produce albums that do not fit the arbitrary criteria set by local censors will be shut out of the distribution system. Major labels won't release albums that they think might not be sold in major outlets. Independent labels are already hard-pressed to find store owners willing to stock their products.

2. Who will set the criteria for the warning labels? How will the terms be defined? Most of the individuals calling for labels point to lyrics that they believe are "offensive" or "indecent." The Supreme Court has spent decades trying to define even the much more restrictive term "obscene." If strictly enforced, record warning codes would require that almost every opera of the past three centuries bear a label. And if not strictly enforced, warning labels are even more outrageously undemocratic.

3. Focusing on the lyrics raises serious questions about precedent. Song lyrics have traditionally been considered poetry, and if children or others are forbidden access to song lyrics, how long will it be before they're forbidden access to certain poems? This is no overstatement: Allen Ginsberg's *Howl*, banned in 1956, was subsequently hailed as one of the finest examples of contemporary American poetry; in 1987, it was banned once again, this time by the FCC, which deemed it too "indecent" for broadcast. What about the erotic poetry of the Bible's "The Song of Solomon"?

RESOURCES

"You've Got a Right To Rock" is a 24-page pamphlet published by *Rock & Roll Confidential*, tracing the history and meaning of the war against rock and offering tips on what to do about it. Available for $3 from RRC, P.O. Box 341305, Los

Angeles, CA 90034.

If major radio stations won't play your music, contact Zoom Black Magic, the only unlicensed radio network in the country. Write them at 8 Kaviland Street, Fresno, CA 93706 or 333 North 12 Street, Springfield, IL 62702.

The No More Censorship Defense Fund, originally established to fight Jello Biafra's censorship bust, still periodically publishes newsletters, fact sheets, and other updates. NMCDF, P.O. Box 11458, San Francisco, CA 94101. Donations requested, nor required.

15
Write and Perform Songs About Free Speech and the Perils of Censorship

Write anti-censorship music and perform it at PTA meetings, city council sessions, on campuses, street corners, etc. Too often, we think we have to be Ice-T or Bruce Springsteen to sing out. But music is such an effective vehicle for communicating human emotion — often the very thing that censors want to repress — that it really needs to be used on every occasion. After all, aren't we fighting a war against enforced silence? (We'll go for peace and quiet after freedom is achieved.)

The Censors' Greatest Hits

This list of great "banned" music of the 20th century does little more than skim the surface. The history of rhythm and blues and rock and roll is littered with more examples — from the banning of such sexual innuendos as Hank Ballard and the Midnighters' "Annie Had a Baby" in the early '50s, to the bowdlerization of MC5's infamous line "Kick out the jams, motherfuckers" in the late '60s, to the ongoing banishment, labeling, and persecution of rap, hip-hop, heavy metal, and other records today.

1. *The Threepenny Opera* and other works, Kurt Weill and Bertolt Brecht

(censored by the Nazis).

2. The works of Dmitri Shostakovich (censored by the Soviet Union).

3. "Goodnight Irene," "Tzena Tzena Tzena," and other hits, the Weavers (censored during the McCarthy era).

4. Elvis Presley (censored by CBS TV in 1956, which showed him only from the waist up on the "Ed Sullivan Show").

5. "Louie Louie," the Kingsmen (censored by the governor of Indiana and others for alleged indecipherable obscenities).

6. "---- Tha Police," N.W.A. (censored by the FBI and law enforcement groups around the U.S.).

7. John Lennon (In the early 1970s, President Richard Nixon, Senator Strom Thurmond, the FBI, and the Immigration and Naturalization Service conspired to deport him because of the revolutionary politics espoused in his songs. Christian groups also tried to censor Lennon in 1966, after he remarked that the Beatles were more popular than Jesus. Others were enraged by the cover of his 1968 album, *Two Virgins*, which showed him and Yoko Ono in the nude.)

8. *As Nasty As They Wanna Be*, and other albums, 2 Live Crew (censored by federal court in Florida, by police in Florida, Texas, Alabama, North Carolina, South Carolina, Georgia, Rhode Island, Pennsylvania, Massachusetts, and elsewhere).

9. The Doors' Jim Morrison (He was arrested in Hollywood, Florida — and hounded to the end of his life by cops from the same police department that would later persecute 2 Live Crew. They alleged that Morrison had exposed his penis onstage.)

10. "Beyond the Realms of Death," and other songs, Judas Priest (censored by civil lawsuit, with government cooperation).

11. "God Save the Queen," the Sex Pistols (banned by British radio during Queen Elizabeth's 1977 Silver Jubilee, for being anti-monarchical.)

12. *Yesterday and Today*, the Beatles (The album's original cover, which featured the Beatles draped in butcher's smocks and holding raw meat and dismembered children's dolls — used to symbolize their record company's chopping up their U.K. albums to squeeze out additional U.S. releases — never appeared in the stores.)

13. *Beggar's Banquet*, the Rolling Stones (In 1969, the group's record label refused to issue the album with its original cover, which was based on men's room graffiti.)

14. "Rainy Day Women #12 & 35," Bob Dylan (widely banned for its refrain "Everybody must get stoned" by radio stations perfectly comfortable playing Frank Sinatra records about boozing).

15. "Suicide Solution," Ozzy Osbourne (censored by civil lawsuit, with government cooperation).

16. "Like A Prayer," Madonna (Her video for the song, which made a statement against racism and in favor of the sexual nature of religious ecstasy, caused her

to lose her endorsement deal with Pepsi-Cola and to become even more of a target of censors like Rev. Donald Wildmon, whose bidding Pepsi obeyed.)

17. "Stagger Lee," Lloyd Price (This traditional blues had to have its lyric scenario rewritten after being censored for "violence" by Dick Clark and other U.S. broadcasters.)

18. "Let's Spend the Night Together," the Rolling Stones (Widely denied airplay by U.S. radio stations, the song was performed on the "Ed Sullivan Show" only after the group agreed to sing the lyric as "Let's spend some *time* together".)

19. "Brown Eyed Girl," Van Morrison (Its original lyric "Making love in the green grass, behind the stadium" was replaced because of fearful broadcasters.)

20. "Locomotive Breath," Jethro Tull (The group's own record company changed its lyrics from "got him by the balls" to "got him by the *fun*," by splicing in material from a different section of the track.)

10 Great Anti-Censorship Songs

1. "Banned in the U.S.A.," 2 Live Crew's answer to their critics.

2. "Jesse Don't Like It," in which Loudon Wainwright III — America's funniest singer/songwriter — presents the only attack on Senator Jesse Helms that also offers a compassionate insight into the character of America's censor-in-chief: "If Jesse don't like it, it don't stay / Get it out of the museum, get it out of there today / Jesse's favorite painting is the one of the clown / With the daisy in his hand and the tear rollin' down."

3. "Fight For Your Right To Party," the Beastie Boys' invitation to using your rights.

4. "Imagine," John Lennon's human rights ballad.

5. "Yakety Yak," the Coasters' teen liberation anthem of the '50. The verses don't deal with censorship but its chorus mocks every censor: "Yakety yak / Don't talk back."

6. "Live to Tell," Madonna's song about the consequences of emotional repression.

7. "Walk This Way," Run-D.M.C. and Aerosmith join up for the first rap/heavy metal fusion and come up with an anthem for nonconformists.

8. "(I Wanna) Testify," George Clinton's pre-funkadelic hit with the Parliaments is one of the all-time great encouragements to defy those who'd silence us.

9. "Everyday People," a 20-years-ahead-of-its-time Sly and the Family Stone song that reminds us why "diff'rent strokes for diff'rent folks" is the only way to live.

10. "Shaddap You Face," Joe Dolce's 1981 novelty smash is an ode for everyone who won't.

16

Write Movie Moguls and Tell Them to Eliminate the MPAA Ratings Code

Write to Jack Valenti, head of the Motion Picture Association of America (MPAA), and to his bosses, the chief executives of the major studios who distribute the majority of all first-run theatrical films shown in the U.S. Tell them that you want an end to the MPAA ratings code, because it prevents Americans from seeing the same films that people in civilized nations in Europe do.

Millions of Americans are convinced that the MPAA code isn't censorship because it's "voluntary." They don't know that the code, adopted in 1966, is the result of years of Hollywood's buckling under to pressure brought by censorship groups; that hundreds of American films are shown in Europe with lines of dialogue, individual shots, and whole scenes that Americans never see; or that the ratings are the result of secret MPAA board meetings, whose anonymous members issue ratings (on the G, PG, PG-13, R, NC-17, X scale) that they never have to justify or even explain. Yet we're supposed to believe that none of this is "censorship" because it's all "voluntary," a system imposed by the industry itself.

Yet who's doing the volunteering? Not the filmmakers. Ask such famous directors as Brian De Palma, Martin Scorsese, Phil Alden Robinson, and Philip Kaufman, whose works are shown in complete form only outside the U.S., if they've been "rated" or "censored."

The American Civil Liberties Union calls the MPAA ratings system "a private combination of power to limit the marketplace of ideas," which is a lawyer's way of saying it's blatant censorship, although without the government's direct involvement. In practice, this is among the worst kinds of censorship, because it means that any proposed film that might not meet MPAA rating standards probably won't be funded, and therefore, it won't be made. This is especially true of any film likely to be rated X, since thousands of theaters will not carry any X-rated movies. (Since

1981, exactly two films out of nearly 1,300 rated were issued with X certificates, because numerous filmmakers were forced to self-censor in order to avoid an X rating.) Any film that displeases the anonymous members of the MPAA board is subject to being whittled down until it *does* meet approval. To reinforce the delusion that they "aren't censors," the MPAA *will* allow the same film to be re-submitted for re-rating, but *won't* tell the filmmakers what they need to change in order to get rid of an X rating.

Since many Americans believe wholeheartedly in the ratings code as a movie evaluator, audiences suffer by missing out on films that they might otherwise have loved, or might not have been offended by, or might have been offended by, but in some inspiring way.

Perhaps the ratings system isn't censorship; perhaps it's Kafka, Orwell, or science fiction. It sure isn't the First Amendment in operation.

Who Rates the Movies?

Nobody really knows who rates the movies. The information released by the MPAA is sketchy — ostensibly to keep its board members from being bribed or otherwise bought off. The few details one can obtain are not encouraging. The board is composed of 10 salaried members. They're appointed by the MPAA, the National Association of Theatre Owners, and the Independent Film Importers and Distributors Association, and serve from one to two years. The MPAA refuses to say how much they are paid, or how they're found. "There are no special qualifications for Board membership," according to the MPAA's literature, "except one must have shared parenthood experience, and one must love movies, must possess an intelligent maturity of judgment." (Given the tangled syntax here, it's tempting to ask what qualifies the other eight.)

We can say who the MPAA board does *not* include: the unions representing directors, actors, writers, and other key creative artists in the movie world, the people who know the most about the art and craft of filmmaking, as opposed to the business of blue-nose appeasement.

In mid-1990, the board comprised seven women and three men, the oldest aged 70, the youngest, 35. The MPAA gives the board members' highest educational attainment (all but one attended college), but no information on the highly relevant questions of race or religious affiliation. For all anybody knows, the board member whose husband's occupation is "M.D., psychoanalyst," could be the wife of Dr. James Dobson, head of the censorship group, Focus on the Family.

When you write your letter, ask Valenti and his bosses to reveal board members' names, or at least more of the pertinent details about these censors: How many minorities are represented? What churches do they attend, and what is the policy of those churches on censorship and the movies? (If they're all atheists, we ought to know that, too.) Who *isn't* considered for board membership? Are there grounds for dismissal? What are they? Demand the public's right to know this information.

WHERE TO WRITE

Jack Valenti, Motion Picture Association of America, 1133 Avenue of the Americas, New York, NY 10036

Write directly to Jack Valenti, since he is the architect of the system, which was put in place after local obscenity prosecutions mushroomed when the even more restrictive Hayes Censorship Board deteriorated in the mid-'60s. Valenti loves this system (he fought the introduction of even a moderate liberalization, the new NC-17 rating, tooth and nail for most of 1990). Explain to him that he's wrong; there is no reason to be gentle.

Write the major studios, to the attention of the CEOs, at the addresses below. Tell 'em to wake up and join the Twentieth Century!

Warner Communications, Inc., 75 Rockefeller Plaza, New York, NY 10020, (212) 484-8000, or 4000 Warner Boulevard, Burbank, CA 91522, (818) 954-6000

Universal Pictures, 445 Park Avenue, New York, NY 10022, (212) 759-7500, or 100 Universal City Plaza, Universal City, CA 91608, (818) 777-1000

MGM/Pathé, 10000 Washington Boulevard, Culver City, CA 90232, (213) 280-6000

21st Century Film Inc., 8200 Wilshire Boulevard, Beverly Hills, CA 90211, (213) 658-3000

Paramount Communications Inc., 15 Columbus Circle, New York, NY 10023, (212) 373-8000, or 5555 Melrose Avenue, Los Angeles, CA 90038, (213) 468-5000

Orion Pictures Corporation, 711 Fifth Avenue, New York, NY 10022, (212) 758-5100, or 1888 Century Park East, Los Angeles, CA 90067, (213) 282-0550

The Samuel Goldwyn Company, 200 West 57th Street, New York, NY 10019, (212) 315-3030, or 10203 Santa Monica Boulevard, Los Angeles, CA 90067, (213) 284-8493

Twentieth Century Fox, 40 West 57th Street, 8th floor, New York, NY 10019, (212) 556-2555, or P.O. Box 900, Beverly Hills, CA 90213, (213) 277-2211

The Walt Disney Company, 500 South Buena Vista, Burbank, CA 91521, (818) 560-5151

Columbia Pictures, Columbia Plaza, Burbank, CA 91505, (818) 954-6000

The Trouble with NC-17

The NC-17 rating was created to allow films with adult themes to be made, exhibited, and advertised without being confused with sex films. (The adult film industry uses X — or more often XXX — as a signal of films showing explicit sexual acts.) It was only instituted in autumn 1990, and within days of its first use groups around the country were claiming that NC-17 films ought to receive the same treatment that X films do. Many theater owners are still hesitant about showing movies with this rating, although the daily newspapers (who, to their First Amendment shame, generally refuse to carry any advertising for X films) seem willing to go along with the system.

In order to make sure that your local theater owners show NC-17 movies, talk to them. Don't let them sidestep the issue; confront it by pointing out that there are more people who want to see grown-up cinema than there are people with picket signs. If a theater still refuses to change its policy, form a group and start a letter-writing and petition campaign (see #33). Prove your point by getting more people involved on the side of liberty than on the side of censorship.

Don't let the pressure die down — the censors won't. Write your local newspaper; call your radio and TV outlets. Make sure they're reporting the issue — both sides of it.

Ultimately, if a theater owner refuses to show worthwhile films no matter what label the MPAA slaps on them, organize a picket line and boycott (see #34).

17
Watch "The Simpsons" and Other Controversial TV Programs

Make a point of watching "The Simpsons" and other controversial television programs. Television, born during the McCarthy era, has never attained any sense of its First Amendment rights. It may be America's most censored medium. Not only is it strictly overseen by the Federal Communications Commission, not only is every program subject to the intense scrutiny of the network's or the cablecaster's own so-called "standards and practices" division (this industry's pseudonym for its censorship bureau), but network TV is also continually subject to the often-arbitrary demographic (and other) stipulations of advertisers and their agents. And in recent years, it's been subject to pressure from the citizen watchdog groups, like the American Family Association (AFA) and the National Coalition on Television Violence (NCTV), which have proliferated.

But you can't just give up on television. It's our primary disseminator of news and entertainment, too important and powerful to ignore no matter how shallow or disinformational the bulk of its content. And anyway, there are all those *exceptions*. It's time to understand what makes a TV show a target.

The War on Bart

Elementary schools in Elk Grove Village and Chicago Heights, Illinois, banned Bart Simpson T-shirts captioned, "I'm Bart Simpson. Who the hell are you?" School administrators objected to the word "hell." In Elk Grove, a second-grader was asked to turn the "hell" shirt inside out for the day and told not to wear it again. The Chicago Heights culprit was 10.

Similar shirts, bearing slogans such as "Underachiever and proud of it, man," have been banned by schools in California and Kentucky. JC Penney even pulled the shirts from its stores.

"I have no comment," said Bart Simpson, in a statement released by Fox Broadcasting. "My folks taught me to respect elementary school principals, even the ones who have nothing better to do than tell kids what to wear. Is it possible elementary school principals have lost their sense of humor?"

Educators (at least the stiff-necked ones who compose the vocal element) have always feared popular culture, but television, which is powerful and ubiquitous, especially stirs their fears. As always, some educators get TV wrong. The shows they believe exalt culture — the vast Anglophilia of PBS, in particular — turn American kids off, make them feel that "culture" is alien, snooty, hostile. The shows our educational establishments want to censor for teaching the wrong values are probably the ones that teach the best.

The current case in point is the Fox network's primetime cartoon "The Simpsons," based on the work of counterculture cartoonist Matt Groening. The center of the storm is the Simpsons' eldest child, Bart —rebellious, as horny as network standards will allow, disrespectful, and defined at a tender age as an "underachiever." What drives the censors nuts is Bart's *attitude*, summarized in the slogan "Underachiever and proud of it, man." Teachers have been known to lecture parents on the damage they can do by letting their kids watch Bart, and to imply publicly and privately that he's the worst role model since Elvis or Nixon or somebody.

Why have kids seized on "Underachiever and proud of it" as a positive slogan? Because it's a way of defining themselves against the expectations and limitations, not just of teachers and parents, but of everybody who might think they're just another lazy, inattentive, bright, but uninspired, brat. By identifying with "Underachiever," kids convert an epithet into a badge of pride. Like so many other censorship targets, Bart the Underachiever sends the message that you have the right to be who you are, not who the system demands that you be.

And Now — A Word to Their Sponsors

Take a tip from the censors themselves and *let the sponsors know you watch controversial programs*. Be sure to tell the sponsor what programs you watch and that if they bow to the demands of pressure groups, you'll switch brands, if not channels. (Don't tell 'em you're going to buy their product if you don't already use it. For that matter, don't buy products you see advertised on TV just 'cause you like the show or the star. Make Nike make good sneakers, not just great Michael Jordan ads.) But do let 'em know that you'll find a way to do without their cans of beans if they make you do without your favorite show or its most irreverent bits of humor and drama. Advertisers are terrified of bad press associated with the shows they sponsor, so tell them you'll organize a boycott if they *support* censorship. And if they call your bluff — FOLLOW THROUGH!

You can send this message by card, letter, mailgram, or telephone. But send it!

RESOURCES

TV Guide, or your local newspaper's TV listings publication, can be more than just a useful way to check time schedules. It can also be a way of checking up on breaking censorship news. *TV Guide*, through its weekly news briefs and occasional feature articles, covers censorship in the TV world particularly closely —but beware: Its always-conservative editorial spin has become pronounced since Rupert Murdoch added the magazine to his empire. *TV Guide* is at your newsstand; subscriptions are available for $35.88 or four monthly payments of $8.97. Call (800) 628-7300 to order. Your newspaper also probably includes some kind of pull-out TV section in its Sunday edition.

Entertainment Weekly, published by Time-Warner, has, since its founding in early 1990, covered television issues well. Its reporting on issues in the industry, as well as its critical analysis, are thorough. It's $58.24 for 52 weekly issues. Write c/o Time Magazine, Customer Service, P.O. Box 60001, Tampa, FL 33660, or call (800) 541-1000.

Variety, *Hollywood Reporter*, and *Broadcasting* are the TV industry's key trade journals. *Broadcasting* focuses completely on radio and TV, but its coverage isn't very daring; *Variety* and *Hollywood Reporter* are more likely to break censorship stories in a way that people outside the industry can understand them. A one-year subscription to *Variety* is $100. Write Weekly Variety, Subscription Department, 5700 Wilshire Boulevard, Suite 120, Los Angeles, CA 90099. *Hollywood Reporter* is $142 a year, $110 for six months, or $75 for Tuesdays-only subscriptions. Write Re: Subscription, P.O. Box 1431, Los Angeles, CA 90078, or call (213) 484-7411. *Broadcasting*, 1705 DeSales Street, NW, Washington, DC 20036, is available at $70 for a one-year and $35 for a six-month subscription. Write to them Re: Subscription, or call (202) 659-2340.

"MTV News" speaks for the MTV cable channel, which is often targeted by censors and conservative media watchdog groups. In response, "MTV News" has become another primary source of information on attempts to censor TV, as well as on attempts to censor rock music. Kurt Loder is a talking head you *can* trust. Watch it as a watchdog for crimes against free speech. Consult your local cable directory for MTV's channel in your area. "MTV News" airs hourly at 10 minutes to the hour, unless shows such as "Club MTV" or "Yo, MTV Raps" are scheduled. "The Week in Rock" also sometimes covers censorship issues. It airs every Saturday at 6 p.m. and Sundays at 1 p.m. and 6:30 p.m. Their phone number is (212) 258-8700.

Write the Networks

People opposed to censorship should make a habit of writing TV networks and sponsors to show support for favorite shows and to fight censorship efforts. Every single letter has an impact. Each of the major networks, including the cable networks, prepares a document that tallies and summarizes every letter it receives about any aspect of its programming. This document is then circulated to all top-level executives.

So write! Keep in mind, though, that form letters have less impact than personally written ones: In the networks' tallies, the form letters are merely counted and totaled at the bottom, but the personally written ones are excerpted and closely read. If you belong to an anti-censorship group, it might still be useful to generate a form letter (Focus on the Family and the American Family Association use them all the time to promote censorship); but the unique ones are still best.

How many letters does it take to make an impact? In the mid-'80s, HBO had about eight million subscribers. The largest number of letters it received about any one program was *42*!

Some Tips

• What shows should you write about?
At the very least, monitor the news or contact anti-censorship organizations to find out what shows are being targeted by censors. If you have time, you should write about any show that you care about.

• What should you say?
Your letter needs to be thoughtful. State what you like about a show, and why. If you know that the show has been targeted by censors, write about why it should not be censored, and what it has to offer that people need to see. For example, a network once obscured a character's sexual preference after it became afraid that a gay character would offend some viewers. If you feel that healthy representations of all sexual orientations on television are important, tell them that. If you don't tell them, no one else will — and your silence helps Wildmon, Dobson, and the others who contend that all the silent Americans agree with them.

• Where should you write?

At least, send your letters to the network that broadcasts the show that's the subject of your letter. But try to send a letter to everyone on this list.

MAJOR NETWORKS

CBS, Inc., Entertainment Division, 51 West 52nd Street, New York, NY 10019, (212) 975-4321

ABC-TV, Audience Information, 30 West 66th Street, New York, NY 10023, (212) 456-7777

NBC-TV, Audience Services, 30 Rockefeller Plaza, New York, NY 10020, (212) 644-2333

Fox Television Stations, Inc., Viewer Services, 205 East 67th Street, New York, NY 10021, (212) 452-3600

If a local network affiliate pulls a nationally broadcast TV show because of pressure from censors, organize a petition drive and fight back (see #33). Because local markets are much smaller, local affiliates respond to form letters and petitions in a way that major networks do not. Petitions should be as specific as possible in their demands, and they should include the name and address of every person who signs. If you cannot organize a petition drive, write your own letter and get your friends and neighbors to do the same. (You need to start a grassroots anti-censorship group — see #35.)

NATIONAL ORGANIZATIONS

Federal Communications Commission, Complaints and Investigations Bureau Chief, Enforcement Division, Mass Media Bureau, 1919 M Street, NW, Washington, DC 20554

National Cable Television Association, Executive Director, 1724 Massachusetts Avenue, NW, Washington, DC 20036, (202) 775-3550

National Association of Broadcasters, President's Office, 1771 N Street, NW, Washington, DC 20036, (202) 429-5300

MTV, President's Office, 1775 Broadway, New York, NY 10019, (212) 713-6400

Because MTV has been targeted by censorship groups and uses its standards and practices committee to coerce record labels to edit videos, and in fact banned Madonna's "Justify My Love" video, you should be certain to write to them if you care about music on television. All too often, the network acts as if it hears only from those who want it to scissor every video it receives. Help change its corporate mentality.

18

Contact Your Local Cable Outlet to Find Out if It's Being Pressured to Censor Its Programming

Contact your cable outlet and find out what kinds of pressure they've come under to censor their various stations — MTV, BET, pay-cable movie services, etc. Even though the cable TV industry has been federally "deregulated," that only means that they're allowed to charge as much as they can get for cable rates (while steering clear of wiring the "lower demographic" poor and minority communities that would dilute their advertising base). As far as the First Amendment is concerned, cable is tightly regulated, not only by its fear of the FCC — which has grown increasingly censorious since the early '80s — but by its terror of local community pressures. In Massachusetts, for instance, complaints from two housewives were enough to get a cable franchise to dump MTV. Even in supposedly liberal New York, the new 1990 cable franchise allows — practically commands — area cable systems to get rid of the sex-oriented programming on community access channels.

Not only cable, but all non-standard broadcasters are harassed. In 1990, a New York–based satellite TV company, Home Dish Only Satellite Network, Inc., was indicted and fined for obscenity by an Alabama court; Home Dish Only, which transmitted uncut sex films, paid a $150,000 fine. It also went out of business — but still had to pay similar fines in New York and Utah. Even worse, the case sent a signal that local prosecutors can enforce the most restrictive "community standards" against any transmissions reaching an area, effectively enforcing the morals of the Bible Belt in the entire U.S.

RESOURCES

You can get the phone number and address of your cable outlet from your bill, or from your cable guide; sometimes it's even listed on your cable box. Such companies are locally franchised, and even though they're almost never closely regulated, they have reason to fear public pressure. Mainly, of course, that pressure comes from groups who want *less* information, fewer ideas, and a narrower point of view to be aired. Let the cable broadcasters know that there's more than one side to that story, and that they'd better make room for it or face a battle come contract renewal time.

You may also want to read:

The Barefoot Channel: Community Television as a Tool for Social Change, by Kim Goldberg (Vancouver: New Star Books, 1990)

Cable Television and the First Amendment, by Patrick Parsons (Lexington, Mass.: Lexington Books, 1987)

19
Join the
American Civil Liberties Union

Become part of a proud history — join the American Civil Liberties Union. From the 1925 *Scopes* trial, in which Clarence Darrow and William Jennings Bryan fought it out over the right to teach Darwinian evolution in American schools, to the 1977 *Skokie* case, in which American Nazis and other controversial groups won the right to march through Skokie, Illinois, as a confirmation of *everyone's* right to peacefully assemble, the ACLU has been in the forefront of the fight to protect constitutional freedoms through the court system.

This is both its glory — many of the most famous court cases in the annals of civil rights could never have been fought, let alone won, without the ACLU — and its most glaring weakness. Since the ACLU deals almost exclusively with court cases, those who want their civil rights are subjected to the often inconvenient reality of being arrested or sued before they can get help. And though the ACLU provides all legal services *pro bono* — free — there are still heavy costs associated with putting a life or business through the court system. Nevertheless, if you're going to fight for your right to party, picket, print, or protest, it's extremely important to know that this group, and its dedicated lawyers, are available for support and, if need be, leadership.

The ACLU, founded in 1920 by Roger Baldwin, has chapters in every state, in Washington, DC, and on about 10 college campuses. In addition to representing those accused of thought crime, or those whose rights have been abused by the system, the organization also files many *amicus curiae* (friend of the court) briefs, in which it argues in favor of expanding civil liberties. The ACLU believes in a literal interpretation of the First Amendment: There should be no abridgment of freedom of speech or of the press — and that means *none*.

In addition to litigation, the ACLU maintains a Washington legislative office which argues for bills that advance civil liberties and opposes those that trample or restrict them. The group has been especially conscientious in opposing such widely misunderstood forms of censorship as movie and record ratings.

The ACLU mainly sustains itself through dues and contributions. Its current membership is 275,000. Annual dues are $20, joint memberships are available to couples for $30 per year, and those with limited incomes may join for $5. Members receive a quarterly newsletter — and of course, a card to carry. Write or call: The American Civil Liberties Union, 132 West 43rd Street, New York, NY 10036; (212) 944-9800.

RESOURCE

Get "What the ACLU has to say about . . . Pornography and the First Amendment," a one-page xerox that intelligently addresses such topics as sexism and pornography, child pornography, and the question of pornography as an incitement to rape and violence. You'll never again be at a loss when someone argues for censorship because pornography might excite somebody who'll hurt somebody else (you'll just point out the many murderers who say they took their cue from the Bible). When child pornography comes up, you'll tell the censors that sexual exploitation is already a crime — making the film or photograph that documents the offense into the criminal is pointless and counterproductive.

20
Join the
Freedom to Read Foundation

The Freedom to Read Foundation (FTRF) was founded in 1969 by the American Library Association. Its main purpose is summarized in its title, but the Foundation also strenuously opposes all forms of censorship. This group has been on the battlefront as long as anybody, and it works with everyone interested in free expression — particularly writers, librarians, and booksellers. The Foundation also offers legal and financial help to censored libraries, librarians, authors, publishers, and booksellers. As a result, it's one of the most respected anti-censorship organizations in America.

Members of the FTRF receive the quarterly *Freedom to Read Foundation News*, which will help persuade you that censorship is not only a hot, high profile national problem, but an insidious, everyday issue, in places small and large. The number of cases in which librarians alone are asked to censor through restricted access to materials and services is astonishing. Book burnings are regular events. It's enough to make you want to do something to put a stop to such shenanigans.

Foundation membership is available to anyone — for $25 per year, $10 for students. For more membership information, write to the Freedom to Read Foundation, 50 East Huron Street, Chicago, IL 60611. Librarians can join the American Library Association itself, which publishes the influential *American Libraries* and the *ALA Journal*, which is one of the most important book reviewing publications in America. First year dues are $38.

21
Stop the Attack on the National Endowment for the Arts

To help combat the attempt to destroy the National Endowment for the Arts, join the National Campaign for Freedom of Expression. The Campaign works primarily among visual artists. It lists eight goals:

1. To protect the First Amendment rights of artists and audiences in every community.
2. To fight against censorship throughout the United States.
3. To promote the political empowerment of artists.
4. To maximize legislative support.
5. To elect supporters to Congress and defeat opponents of freedom of expression.
6. To form alliances on this issue within and outside the arts.
7. To increase public understanding, not only of the fundamental role that freedom of expression plays in our society, but also of the danger inherent in censorship, in both general and specific instances.
8. To increase funding for the arts for all sectors.

Membership in the Campaign is $15 for individuals, $50 for organizations. Contact the group at P.O. Box 50245, Washington, DC 20004; (202) 393 ARTS. Because it is a political lobbying organization, contributions are not tax-deductible.

"Banned" Art

(All references in this list, unless otherwise noted, are from *Art Censorship: A Chronology of Proscribed and Prescribed Art*, by Jane Clapp [Metuchen, NJ: Scarecrow Press, 1972].)

THE RATIONALIZATION

387 B.C. "Plato counted art as a form of imitation and classed the artist with the sophist — as a maker of images against whom the government must be on its guard . . ."

© 1990 BY STEPHEN KRONINGER.

322 B.C.   "Aristotle urged that special care be taken to protect the immature from pictures as well as talk and books . . ."

IN PRACTICE

1488   The painting *Adam and Eve* by Baccio Bandinelli shocked members of the clergy and was removed from its place behind the altar of a Florence cathedral.

1573   Veronese was accused of sacrilege by the Tribunal of the Holy Office for his painting *The Last Supper that Jesus Took with His Apostles in the House of Simon*. The Inquisitors were offended because Veronese included "German pikemen, servants, a dwarf, jesters, a parrot, [and] a dog" alongside the Holy figures. The artist refused to make any substantial changes in the work, but he did change the title to *Feast in the House of Levi*.

1605   Caravaggio's *Maddona del Serpe* (*Madonna of the Serpent*) was removed from the Pala Frenierei because the figures of Mary and the Christ Child were "indecently portrayed."

1863   Edouard Manet's *Dejeuner sur l'Herbe* (*Luncheon on the Grass*) "seemed to be a signal for the condemnation of the whole group of Impressionists in the name of morality." (Germain Bazin, in *The Avant-Garde in Painting*, Simon & Schuster, New York, 1969.)

1875   Auguste Rodin was accused by fellow artists of using a life cast for his sculpture *Age d'Airain* (*Age of Bronze*). The work, a male nude, was subsequently withdrawn from the show where it was being exhibited.

1896   Frederick MacMonnies's *Baccante and Infant Faun* was described by Harvard art professor Charles Eliot Norton as "a naked woman dancing in her shame" and "inebriate and blatantly licentious". A subsequent petition drive led to its removal from the Boston Public Library.

1898   Käthe Kollwitz's *The Weavers*, a set of six prints inspired by a textile workers' strike, won a Gold Medal at a prestigious art show in Berlin. The work was hailed as "a landmark of socially conscious art," but the prize was vetoed by Kaiser Wilhelm II, who called it "gutter art."

1917   Art Young's cartoon "Having Their Fling" was used as evidence by the U.S. Government in its case against *The Masses*, a socialist monthly. The cartoon, which had appeared in the magazine, showed four figures (labeled "editor," "capitalist," "politician," and "minister") dancing under a shower of gold pieces, presumably the spoils of World War I. Seven members of the magazine's staff were charged with "obstructing the war effort."

1969   A poster depicting Michelangelo's *David* was confiscated from a bookstore in Sydney, Australia. The store's manager was charged with obscenity.

COMING TO THE RESCUE

In 1954, a statement issued by the Board of Trustees of the American Federation of Arts warned that "freedom of artistic expression in a visual work of art, like freedom of speech and press, is fundamental in our democracy" and that "this fundamental right exists irrespective of the artist's political or social opinions, affiliations, or activities".

22
Join Article 19

Article 19 is a human rights group working to identify and oppose censorship around the world. It's especially important for Americans critical of our government and censorship system to participate, because in many countries the government justifies its censorship practices by saying, "They do it in America, the freest country in the world." So let 'em know *it's not free enough*.

Article 19 is based on Article 19 of the United Nations Universal Declaration of Human Rights (ratified by many nations, honored in full by none), which declares: "Everyone has the right to freedom of opinion and expression; this right includes freedom to hold opinions, without interference, and to seek, receive, and impart information and ideas through any media regardless of frontiers."

Dues are $19, yearly. Applications and information are available from Article 19, International Centre on Censorship, 90 Borough High Street, London SE1 1LL, England.

23
Support the
American Booksellers Association
Foundation for Free Expression

The American Booksellers Association Foundation for Free Expression works through American bookstores to support free speech and to turn back censorship. Formed in June 1990 at the annual ABA convention, it is led by the well-respected Oren Teicher, who is also the ABA's associate executive director. Its mission is "to inform and educate booksellers, other members of the book industry, and the public about the deleterious effects of censorship; to actively promote and protect the free expression of ideas, particularly freedom in the choice of reading material." The Foundation circulates a poster that has also been used as an advertisement, which included a "ballot," i.e., a petition coupon. The poster features "An uncensored letter to America's readers," written by ABA president Ed Morrow and Harry Hoffman, president and CEO of Walden Book Co., the publishing industry's largest retail chain. It reads, in part:

> "We believe attempts to censor the ideas to which we have access —whether in books, magazines, plays, works of art, television, movies, or song — are not simply isolated instances of harassment by diverse special interest groups. Rather, they are part of a growing pattern of increasing intolerance, which is changing the fabric of America. . . . Censorship cannot eliminate evil. It can only kill freedom. We believe Americans have the right to buy, stores have the right to sell, authors have the right to write and publishers have the right to publish Constitutionally-protected material. Period."

When this open letter/petition was first published in 28 American newspapers, more than 76,000 people responded by signing and returning the ballots to the ABA.

To sign and/or circulate the petition, contact the ABA at P.O. Box 672, New York, NY 10113; (212) 463-8450. To get their new set of four "freedom of expression" posters, send a check for $10.

24
Get to Know the Censorship Groups; Study Their Literature, and Expose Them to Public Scrutiny

Know your enemy. Contact pro-censorship groups like the American Family Association, the Parents' Music Resource Center, Focus on the Family, and other censorship groups. Study their literature and publicize and propagandize to expose its lies and fallacies.

See your enemies for who they are, not for what they profess to the media. Doing that can be tricky, though. The strategies, as well as the goals, of the pro-censorship groups are often covert and dishonest.

Try to get your name placed on the groups' mailing lists and review the materials they send out (which often arrive on a monthly basis). Call and represent yourself as a researcher; that's what you are doing. Or call and speak to them as a concerned parent, student, teacher, law enforcement officer, or book/record buyer, if you're any of those. You don't have to lie, just be as selective as possible about stating your viewpoint.

Make sure you keep documentation of the materials you receive and what you find out. Tape recordings, letters, brochures, and other materials may help you uncover information that the censors didn't want us to know.

The real story is often in the connections you're not supposed to make. The wife of U.S. Secretary of State James Baker sits on FOF's board, but no one is supposed to question this fact, and no one dares ask whether the Secretary of State is himself a Dobsonite. (Actually, we did ask, and were told, "No comment.")

Groups to Contact

Focus on the Family (FOF), 801 Corporate Center Drive, Pomona, CA 91768, (714) 620-8500

Perhaps the largest and most dangerous censorship group today, FOF publishes an influential monthly magazine, *Focus on the Family Citizen*, which frequently attacks rock records (its favorite target), as well as comic books, TV shows, films, and school textbooks. *Focus on the Family Citizen* boosts the American Family Association's media boycotts, the shameful anti-abortion tactics of Randall Terry, Phyllis Schlafly's anti-feminist Eagle Forum, and a slew of other evangelical activities, including those of convicted Watergate conspirator Charles Colson.

Leader James Dobson is not a minister but he is a fundamentalist Christian "family values" counselor who has preached against "parental permissiveness" since the '60s. FOF is also anti-abortion, pro–school prayer, anti-evolution, and wary of too much information about the Holocaust getting out. Its board of directors includes Susan Baker, wife of U.S. Secretary of State James Baker, and co-founder of the Parents' Music Resource Center. Articles in FOF's *Citizen* sicced the cops on rap group N.W.A. for the song "---- Tha Police," resulting in a national effort to prevent the group from performing live, and the FBI's involvement in the case.

American Family Association (AFA), P.O. Drawer 2440, Tupelo, MS 38803, (601) 844-5036

The Reverend Donald Wildmon's anti-pornography crusade through the AFA is, in fact, a vehicle for censorship, frequently advocating boycotts of sponsors of TV shows it considers "anti-Christian," motel chains it believes show "pornographic" (i.e., R-rated) movies, and the like. Wildmon orchestrated the campaign that successfully severed Pepsi's sponsorship ties to Madonna because of "Like A Prayer," her supposedly "blasphemous" video, and was at the center of the campaign against Martin Scorsese's film, *The Last Temptation of Christ*. Wildmon's statements about the management of Universal Studios during the latter campaign, along with his publication of a survey on how many Jews work in Hollywood, earned him condemnation as an anti-Semite from, among others, the Roman Catholic Archbishop of St. Louis, the head of the Mennonite church, and the head of one Lutheran synod. Wildmon wasn't just central to the Jesse Helms–led attack on the National Endowment for the Arts — he started it, with a mailing list attack on artist Andres Serrano's photo *Piss Christ*. Wildmon is currently being sued for copyright infringement for using without permission a detail from the work of artist David Wojnarowicz in his anti-NEA literature.

Working through such offshoots and affiliates as the National Federation for Decency (NFD) and CLeaR-TV (Christian Leaders for Responsible Television), Wildmon boasts of having prevented CBS from basing a cartoon series on the Garbage Pail Kids, and of spending $50,000 campaigning for 1988's ultra-repressive Child Protection and Obscenity Enforcement Act. Wildmon also came up with the bizarre allegation that the Saturday morning cartoon character Mighty Mouse encouraged cocaine sniffing by his habit of basking in the aroma of flowers. A sane nation would have laughed boisterously; this one allowed censors to force Mighty Mouse to cease and desist.

Because Wildmon is regarded by many as a loose cannon, more respectable types tend to shy away from direct identification with him. One of his publications reprinted a chapter from Tipper Gore's rock-bashing book, *Raising PG Kids in an X-Rated World*, with the publisher's permission. When this was revealed,

Senator Al Gore was forced to issue a statement denying any association with Wildmon and condemning his anti-Semitism. Yet the press rarely mentions this aspect of Wildmon's act; the *New York Times Magazine* ran an October, 1990, cover story slamming the guy without ever mentioning it. As a result, the threat of a Wildmon boycott often intimidates advertisers. In November 1990, Burger King announced that it was withdrawing its commercials from several TV shows to which Wildmon's CLeaR-TV objected. The same week, CLeaR-TV called off a boycott of Burger King.

Parents' Music Resource Center (PMRC), 1500 Arlington Boulevard, Arlington,
VA 22209, (703) 527-9466

The PMRC was formed in 1984 as a "housewives group" — in fact, by the wives of 15 senators, congressmen, and Cabinet officials along with a couple of DC businessmen's spouses. Allegedly attacking only "irresponsible" rock music and lobbying only for "consumer information," it, in fact, displays a consistent Christian evangelical bias: For instance, the PMRC originally wanted record warning labels to bear an "O" for those with "occult" material (an infringement of religious freedom). It virtually never speaks of the positive side of music it attacks. Notoriously deceitful with the press, the PMRC frequently claims allies it does not have (Bruce Springsteen, the American Pediatric Association), and continually denies ties with censors further right. Its leaders are Tipper Gore, wife of Tennessee's senator Al Gore, and Susan Baker, wife of the Secretary of State and herself a Focus on the Family board member. Through such ties, and its endorsement of much of the looniest literature in the field, the PMRC is the crucial link between the relatively respectable censors and the really frightening guys mumbling in the corner on the far right.

Jack Thompson, P.O. Box 73, Coral Gables, FL 33114, (305) 666-4366

An attorney connected to both FOF and the AFA, Jack Thompson stirred the national witchhunt against rappers 2 Live Crew (whose record company had opposed his candidacy for political office). He operates out of his house with a phone and a fax machine. With his strict Christian fundamentalist world view, he claims he's saving the souls of the groups he vilifies. Thompson says he does not favor censorship, just strict enforcement of obscenity laws. Told CBS television he believes 2 Live Crew belongs in prison.

Eagle Forum, P.O. Box 618, Alton, IL 62002, (618) 462-5415

Founded by Phyllis Schlafly, this anti-feminist, anti-abortion, anti–sex education, ultra-right group, came into prominence as the women's group that most vigorously opposed the Equal Rights Amendment. It aids the PMRC in actions against live rock concerts; successfully lobbied for the San Antonio anti–rock concert legislation; and helped inflame legislatures in Florida, Missouri, and Tennessee against pop music lyrics. Tipper Gore of the PMRC has run an anti-rock "workshop" for them, which created a cadre of anti-lyrics lobbyists including Shirley Marvin of Missouri Project Rock and Carol Griffin, Florida's "Key Eagle."

Wants to see "creation theory" in textbooks. Eagle Forum publishes the *Phyllis Schlafly Report* (monthly; $15 a year).

Bob Larson's Ministries, P.O. Box 26A, Denver, CO 80236, (800) 223-2582; (303) 980-1511; (303) 980-6555

Nationally syndicated radio talk show host Bob Larson purveys many fundamentalist ideas, including the idea that most modern entertainment is immoral and that pop music, in particular, is satanic. Claiming to have been a rock musician himself in the early '60s, Larson has been on the attack since '66.

Truth About Rock Ministries, P.O. Box 9222, North St. Paul, MN 55109, (612) 770-8114

Through their Truth About Rock Ministries, ordained ministers Dan and Steve Peters specialize in conducting record album burnings, traveling around the country from their Minnesota base to conduct bonfires that whip congregations into an anti–pop culture froth. Their book, *Why Knock Rock*, is a distressingly popular how-to/why-to guide to album burning. The Peters condemn rock stars for non-Christian religious beliefs: Tina Turner, for instance, is attacked as a Buddhist, Seals and Crofts as Bahais. Dan Peters has also stated that the Jewish star (the Star of David) is the "universal symbol of Satan."

Back in Control Training Center, 1234 West Chapman, Suite 203, Orange, CA 92668, (714) 538-2563

The self-proclaimed "de-punking/de-metaling" group, Back in Control Training Center is run by two former Los Angeles probation officers. The group's training manual, allegedly in use in several California police departments, accuses several rock stars of occult involvement. Back in Control's original list of "satanic symbols" included the peace sign ("an upside down broken cross to mock Christianity") and the Jewish star ("Hexagram: six-pointed star representing the Jewish star of David"). The latter was begrudgingly changed after too much bad press. It's a great place for information on why your kid is devil-inhabited, right down to the T-shirts and sneakers. Endorsed in Tipper Gore's book and other PMRC literature.

Summit Ministries, 108 Mohawk Avenue, P.O. Box 207, Manitau Springs, CO 80829, (719) 685-9103

David Noebel of Summit Ministries was one of the first anti–rock music crusaders. As early as 1965, in books such as *The Marxist Minstrels, Rhythm, Riots and Revolution*, and *Communism, Hypnotism and The Beatles*, he attacked Dylan and the Beatles as part of a plot by the Marxist anti-christ. According to Noebel, the whole thing's a Communist conspiracy and if we don't get rock off the radio and record store shelves, "Degenerated Americans will indeed raise the Communist flag over their own nation." Noebel's racism is muted but clear: In *Folk Music and the Negro Revolution*, he states that in Africa, rock was played while natives boiled people in pots, that Martin Luther King was a Communist, and that the civil rights movement was in fact nothing more than a front for a giant orgy of miscegenation, with the Voting Rights Act a plot "to turn the South into a Negro Soviet America."

700 Club, CBN Center, Centerville Turnpike and Indian River Road, Virginia Beach, VA 23463, (804) 424-7777; (804) 523-7000; Prayer line: (804) 420-0700

Televangelist Pat Robertson and his 700 Club survived the great broadcast preacher scandals of 1988 unscathed, despite revelations of cowardice during his Korean War service, which emerged in his presidential campaign. Robertson often uses "700 Club" broadcasts as a forum for religious intolerance, complaining about "Buddhism, Hinduism, and all the other 'isms'." Robertson's "700 Club" co-host, Sheila Walsh, sits on the PMRC's advisory board. She "reviews" records about which the group receives inquiries — but does not listen to them.

National Organization for Women (NOW), 1000 16th Street, NW, Washington, DC 20036, (202) 331-0066

The National Organization for Women consistently adopts pro-censorship positions on subjects ranging from Bret Easton Ellis's novel *American Psycho* to Bruce Springsteen's use of the word "girl" in his song lyrics. Always careful to couch its advocacy of censorship in pseudoliberal rhetoric, in fact, NOW uses essentially the same tactics as right-wing anti-feminists. NOW is not the government. NOW doesn't advocate prior restraint. NOW has not adopted a national position on these issues. What this really means is that NOW wants to be let off the hook because it represents a vulnerable constituency. It also means that national leaders like the organization's nominal leader, Molly Yard, are continually subordinate to localized zealots like Tammy Bruce, the leader of the Los Angeles chapter, and an organizer of the attacks on *American Psycho*.

Women Against Pornography (WAP), 358 West 47th Street, New York, NY 10036, (212) 307-5505

Feminist freedom fighters? Or just a particular form of censor? Women Against Pornography rabidly protects the rights of women, but in the process it avidly tramples all over the First Amendment. The totally censorious effect of the "anti-pornography" laws the group helped introduce in Minneapolis and Indianapolis in the mid-'80s can be gauged by the fact that all the most right-wing censorship groups, including the AFA and Focus on the Family, also supported their passage. WAP has abandoned the idea of educating Americans about nonsexist behavior in favor of rendering illegal not just behavior, but all manner of opinion with which it disagrees.

Parent Teacher Association (PTA), 700 North Rush Street, Chicago, IL 60611, (312) 787-0977

The national PTA will *tell* you it opposes censorship, and when it comes to books, the group is sometimes helpful. But its position on popular culture, particularly rock music, is atrocious. The group had a position paper on rock lyrics before it bothered to adopt one on what many find to be the more pressing issue of illiteracy.

of illiteracy.

Join your local PTA. Work with other parents to make sure that your local PTA sends the national headquarters a strong message in favor of free expression.

Public Broadcasting System (PBS), 1320 Braddock Place, Alexandria, VA 22314, (703) 739-5000

Disregarding public television's mandate "to reflect the community as a whole, in all its diversity," PBS's structure and timidity foster programming that mirrors the community that can afford it. While PBS management has not shied away from censoring points of view or subject matters on its own, the economics of public broadcasting also serve that purpose well.

Funding for PBS comes from three sources: government, corporations and foundations, and viewer subscriptions. While government money tends to come with strings (i.e., satellite money for satellite time) and audience money goes primarily to station upkeep (utilities, salaries, etc.), corporations donate money connected to specific programming, either in pieces or in full sponsorship. So while "The MacNeil/Lehrer News Hour," which demonstrably favors the center-right end of the political spectrum, hasn't a stressful moment with its $10 million per year AT&T underwriting (nearly half of its total budget), GlobalVision's left-of-center "South Africa Now" was eviscerated when its limited foundation donations dried up, as was investigative journalist Jonathan Kwitny's liberal "The Kwitny Report." By contrast, conservative programs like Morton Kondrake's "American Interests" and William Buckley's "Firing Line" have few worries, since they are underwritten entirely by right-wing foundations and corporate interests.

Alternate points of view seem to terrify PBS. *Days of Rage*, a sympathetic documentary about the Palestinian intifada, was smothered by discussion panels that were longer than the movie.

A radically restructured funding system is the only way for PBS to clean the mud off its image as a genuine public broadcaster.

National Coalition on Television Violence (NCTV), P.O. Box 2157, Champaign, IL 61825, (217) 384-1920

The National Coalition on Television Violence (NCTV) represents the height of censorship pseudoscience. Thomas Radeki has made his group the statisticians of anti-violence; figures and percentages flow heavily, though without much context. It's a great plan as long as you think that all violence is created equal —that is, that the differences between the violence in a Tom and Jerry cartoon, a *Rambo* movie, and a miniseries about child abuse are matters of "how often" rather than "what kind."

NCTV's real agenda is to define a spurious category — "violence" — which is always and inevitably a bad thing, and a category to which free speech doesn't apply. Unfortunately, Radeki and NCTV — as well as allies such as the notorious, pseudo–ordinary housewife (actually a wealthy, Mormon member of the Michigan Council of the Arts) Terry Rakolta, who stirred the campaign against Fox TV's "Married with Children" —have found willing listeners for their folderol at such publications as *TV Guide and the New York Times.*

25
Investigate the Tax-Exempt Status of Pro-Censorship Lobbying Groups

Investigate the tax-exempt status of groups that lobby Congress and other legislative institutions for censorship regulations. Ask elected officials, newspapers, and other media outlets to do the same.

Nonprofit groups must register with the federal government to be granted tax-exempt status under section 501(c)(3) of the Internal Revenue Code. Such status is granted only to groups with charitable or religious purposes. The tax exemption can be removed if the group is found to be, in fact, a lobbying or political-activist organization. (Although this provision is never applied to religious groups that, for instance, instruct their congregations not to vote for people advocating certain policies — on abortion, for instance — as long as the instruction is done by innuendo.) Rules on lobbying are more strictly applied, however, and some organizations may be vulnerable to challenge on this basis. You probably need to consult an attorney, preferably one experienced in dealing with nonprofit groups, to put this idea into action.

While restrictions may vary slightly from state to state, all groups that do fund-raising are generally required to register with the secretary of state in each state in which they solicit — even if that solicitation is done by mail or telephone. Furthermore, all such groups are usually also *required to file a tax return in every state in which they conduct fund-raising.* And many groups don't bother, either because they don't know or because they figure nobody's paying attention. Pay attention.

Contact your Department of State's Office of Charities and Registrations (that's what it's called in New York; the agency's name may vary elsewhere). Request the financial statement of the group in which you are interested. You may need to learn the legal name of the organization, as it may be different from its commonly used one. Check the group's literature to see if there is a separate entity that, for instance, holds the copyright to that literature.

If the group is not registered *and on file* with your state, file a complaint. It is likely that the group in question is illegally soliciting funds.

But that's only where the fun begins. If the group *is* registered, their financial records must show a variety of information, including the names of all officers and the names of all large contributors. Many groups do their best to keep alliances with high-powered executives and politicians secret. Such public filings are one of the few ways in which hidden connections come to light.

Scour the information you receive; look not only for prominent names but for names connected to prominent names. For instance, Susan Baker, the wife of the U.S. Secretary of State, James Baker, is on the board of directors of Focus on the Family. This is worth inquiring about: Does it mean that Secretary Baker wants to deny women abortion rights, put prayer back in school, prevent the teaching of evolution — and gut the First Amendment to fit fundamentalist requirements? These are important questions, and Baker's refusal to publicly address them makes exposing the connection much more significant.

26
Find Out
Your State's Requirements for
Purchasing Textbooks

What are your state's requirements for purchasing textbooks? If you watch late night reruns of *Inherit the Wind*, it will seem odd that anyone could have ever gotten so worked up about something as basic to modern science as the notion of Darwinian evolution. The idea that a teacher went to court over the right to teach science seems even more dated. But the sad truth is that today's educators are running scared, desperately avoiding public conflict, even on issues that come as close to fact as anything known — Darwinian evolution chief among them.

There were 172 reported incidences of attempted textbook censorship in 42 states during 1989; the American Library Association reports that there were at least 1,000 cases of textbook "challenges" in one year alone (1989-90).

The problem is more extreme in states where school systems must purchase textbooks from lists provided by the state. Such lists are determined after public hearings. Textbook hearings have been used as opportunities to lobby for the inclusion of such scientifically dubious items as "creationism." That's the theory that the Biblical account of the earth's creation as set down in Genesis is historically accurate and, perhaps more important, that Darwinian evolution does not occur but is a mere hypothesis. That is a "theory" in the crudest sense. (For a refutation of creationism, and similar misconceptions, read Stephen Jay Gould's 1981 book *The Mismeasure of Man*.)

Creationists have targeted large states like California and Texas for textbook challenges because they are huge markets and their standards help determine what texts get published in the first place. In California, which leads the nation in the number of science textbook challenges, the state requires full coverage of evolution but it is no longer permissible to call the Darwinian world view "science fact." In Texas, until recently, only *objections* to texts could be heard, which meant that those who agreed with conventional science had no chance to speak. In that climate, such anti-evolutionists as Mel and Norma Gabler of the creationist Education Research Analysts became inordinately powerful; despite recent changes in Texas law, the Gablers remain heavily influential.

If the Gablers wanted only to ensure that creationism received attention in textbooks, they would simply be exercising First Amendment rights of their own. But they want to dictate a variety of textbook topics. For instance, they oppose teaching about the Great Depression of the 1930s because it "will only succeed in raising doubts about our system," and contend that a history text with references to Rosa Parks, the woman who sparked the Montgomery, Alabama, bus boycott in the 1950s, places excessive emphasis on "the minorities." The Gablers attack material that they believe contains references to "secular humanism," "values clarification," and "New Age religion." Their emphasis isn't on getting their ideas heard; it's on silencing those they disagree with, up to and including banning the study of archeology, slavery, the Watergate scandal, the

Equal Rights Amendment, and even pollution. The Gablers have said: "As long as the schools continue to teach abnormal attitudes and alien thoughts, we caution parents not to urge their children to pursue high grades and class discussion, because the harder students work, the greater their chance of brainwashing."

The Gablers aren't alone, of course. Phyllis Schlafly of Eagle Forum wants to outlaw international studies and prevent American students from being told that they are "citizens of the world . . . and that we are interdependent." She also labeled a course on the Holocaust "too controversial." Apparently, teaching young Americans about the activities of Hitler youth is a form of "child abuse." Eagle Forum also works closely with Citizens for Excellence in Education (CEE), an offshoot of the National Association of Christian Educators, which was involved in 22 censorship incidents in 1987-88. CEE is often cited by parents who want books removed from reading lists.

It's not only the sciences that are threatened. Concerned Women for America (CWA), headed by Beverly LaHaye, whose husband co-founded the Moral Majority, believes: "All children have lost their First Amendment right to attend school without having their religious beliefs attacked, ridiculed, and undermined." CWA opposes using *The Diary of Anne Frank* in the classroom because the diary of a young woman murdered in the Holocaust implies that all religions are equally valid. Supernaturalism was cited as a reason for banning *The Wizard of Oz*, *Cinderella*, and *King Arthur*.

Censorship groups have failed in their attempts to ban books in Florida, Alabama, and Louisiana. But the No More Censorship Defense Fund estimates that the censors win more than one-third of the time. In addition, textbooks are being written to avoid controversy, and that means many important subjects are slighted. "One topic that often gets shortchanged is the study of comparative religions," points out No More Censorship. "History is full of examples of how religion has, for better or worse, influenced events and yet contemporary texts generally fail to mention or examine the religious motivations of the Pharaohs, the Crusades, or the Pilgrims. Students inevitably get a flawed perspective on history, not unlike their Soviet peers."

One way you can help is to find out what the rules are. If your school board does not have a concrete school materials selection policy, offer to help formulate one. Help make sure that the policy works to protect minority interests — otherwise you'll only create more destructive red tape than is already in place.

RESOURCES

Censorship and Selection: Issues and Answers for Schools, by Henry F. Reichman. Shows how to develop viable policies ranging from how to handle censorship complaints to how to select learning materials. Specific recommendations on how schools and libraries can plan for potential crises are also available. $12.95 from the American Library Association, 50 East Huron Street, Chicago, IL 60611; (312) 944-6780.

"Censorship or Selection: Choosing Books for Public Schools." An hour-long videotape from Columbia University's esteemed journalism school, shows a 22-member panel discussion on how books get into classrooms and libraries —and how they're sometimes removed. You can create your own program or get your local TV station to show this one. $150 from Media and Society Seminars, Graduate School of Journalism, Columbia University, New York, NY 10027.

The Center for Civic Education, 5146 North Douglas Fir Road, Calabasas, CA 91302; (818) 340-9320. Develops curriculum materials to teach high school students about the Constitution.

27
Run for Office on a Platform Supporting Freedom of Expression

Running for office is a drastic step, but hardly an impossible one. After all, you're not going to run for president, you're going to run for an office (probably) held by a small-time Mickey Mouse politician with a bad attitude about the First Amendment — your local city council, school board, or state legislature. And you're going to act out the real dream of democracy: You're going to give people *a real choice*.

You DON'T need a million bucks, the permission or endorsement of any political party, or a slick, big budget advertising campaign. And you sure don't need to apologize for running on this issue — running to protect free speech is just as fundamental to the conception of America as, say, running to lower taxes.

You DO need the conviction that you're right about the issue, a clear understanding of its roots, extensions, and implications, and some kind of base in the community in which you're running. Plus you'll need the filing fee, which is probably no more than $100. Some areas that are into making democracy really difficult also require petitions signed by a specified number of voters registered in the area in which the election is being held. It helps to have some kind of visible local reputation, but it isn't essential — and anyway, running for office on a First Amendment platform in a censored area will *make* you notorious.

Still sound farfetched? Well, heed the story told by Michael "Supe" Granda, bassist for the Ozark Mountain Daredevils. In the late '80s, his hometown, Springfield, Missouri, was afflicted by the presence of State Representative Jean Dixon. Dixon inaugurated the nationwide push for record labeling, and harassed local university officials who were attempting to stage *The Normal Heart*, Larry Kramer's play about the AIDS crisis. First Supe got annoyed; then he got busy, deciding to run against Dixon in the state's Republican primary. Here's Supe's account.

As a traveling musician, I'm often asked where I come from. I use two major signposts: (1) It is located halfway between the Atlantic and Pacific Oceans, and (2) It is located halfway between Canada and Mexico. Pressed further, I use the following simple description: During the Civil War, Missouri was a neutral state. Let's start there.

Living in the "middle of nowhere" has both advantages and disadvantages. Of course there is the clean air and the clean water, but unfortunately, along with this pastoral beauty comes an attitude among many of the people that I will describe only as "less than open-minded." After all, Springfield, Missouri, is the world headquarters of the Assembly of God churches, making it the "official buckle" of the Bible Belt.

It was this attitude that prompted me, a lazy musician, to get off my couch and do whatever I could to help stem a very gaudy display of less-than-open-minded extremism that was being exhibited in the Missouri House of Representatives. Rep. Jean Dixon and her ever-growing group of God-intoxicated followers were not only offending my sensibilities, their stance on censorship could directly affect my livelihood.

Having spent the first 39 years of my life paying little or no attention to the political arena, I hadn't the slightest idea about what could be done. Nor did I have the slightest clue about how to go about doing it. I picked up my phone and dialed the number of the representative from an adjacent district, who just happened to be a music fan and *younger* than I was.

Through him, I found that all a citizen of Missouri has to do to run for a seat in the House of Representatives is make a personal appearance in the Office of the Secretary of State, prove you reside in the district in which you intend to run, and pay $50. Other states may require additional criteria. In Missouri, it is absurdly simple.

The 135-mile trek to Jefferson City was made on a sunny spring day, the kind of day that makes one glad he lives in Missouri. After a leisurely three-hour drive through the beautiful Ozark countryside, the actual filing procedure took all of three minutes. The time was well spent, and the 50-dollar bill I took out of my pocket was a small price to pay for what I thought I must do, and in order to say what I must say, as a responsible citizen of this state AND this country.

Objections to music are nothing new. My father hated the Rolling Stones, as they sang about spending the night together, probably as much as his father complained when Frank Sinatra sang about getting drunk and getting laid. Modern day music and its message isn't any more of a threat to us now than it was to the caveman who objected to the racket his neighbor made while banging two rocks together.

My decision to run for office was sane and sober. I wanted to use my name and what status I had acquired in my community to represent those of us (middle-aged lovers of rock 'n' roll music) who are intelligent enough to make decisions for ourselves and our children. To allow people like Dixon to decide what my kids can and can't do, or listen to, was too much for me to take lying down.

When the media got wind of my actions, I was caught up in an immediate whirlwind of activity. My phone rang off the wall; everyone wanted to know why I was doing what I was doing, and was I really serious about it. In a matter of days, everyone in Springfield was aware of what I was doing.

I had no huge aspiration to be elected to office. What constituency would willingly elect a musician with a studio tan and hair to his waist? My only object was to inform as many people as I could that the incumbent's views were dangerous and that we should think about not making the same mistake twice and re-electing her.

I'm proud to reside in Missouri. The people are aware of the country we live in, as well as the planet we live on, and I was insulted as my representative depicted us as a group of simpletons, unable to think for ourselves.

The right of all candidates to "equal time" was afforded me, and every time we were warned of satanic intervention by Dixon, I was able to present the other side of the story, the side that says the world isn't going to end just because someone, somewhere, wants to say "doo-doo" into a microphone.

As I conducted my campaign, prominent people of the community came out of the woodwork to congratulate me on my actions and pledge their support and money. I was also warned of the age-old political practice of "voter pool dilution." I entered the campaign as an intelligent person and immediately realized that if I were to capture a mere 200 votes, allowing Dixon to win re-election by a margin of 150, not only would I have defeated my own purpose, I would have come off looking like an idiot, having just shot myself in the foot.

Before I'd even entered the second week of my campaign, I realized I wasn't going to be able to continue to the end. On the last day for a candidate to officially withdraw his name from the ballot, I called a news conference. I alerted all the media in town that I was going to issue a statement at the very traditional "high noon in the rotunda of the court house." I considered it quite a compliment that they deemed my actions worthy of their attention, their time, and their presence.

I carefully prepared and read my statement, so as not to stumble over words or thoughts, leading to misquotation. I kept the statement quick and to the point, informing everyone that I was driving back to Jefferson City, where I intended to withdraw from the race. I urged all those who supported me to throw their support to Connie Wybel, a third candidate and a fellow opponent of Dixon.

Through the course of the summer, I kept a high profile. The outcome was the successful ousting of Jean Dixon. In the process, I taught myself a valuable lesson: I learned that every little bit helps and even though my contribution to the cause may have been quite minute, that gulp of champagne on election night was mighty sweet.

Yes, you *can* make a difference.

28
Write to Your Favorite Artists; Find Out What They're Doing to Help Preserve Freedom of Expression

Write to your favorite artists — in any field — and ask what they're doing to help preserve free expression. Find out if *they* have been harassed and what you can do to help stop it. Write authors in care of their publishers, movie stars in care of the video companies that have issued their most recent film on videotape, recording artists at their record companies. Addresses of these companies are on the package. Visual artists can be reached in care of the galleries that show their work.

Allen Ginsberg, one of America's greatest living poets and a writer often censored for the explicit language and imagery of his best works, wrote the following statement to the Federal Communications Commission. He wrote the statement in 1990, after the FCC banned all "indecency" — 24 hours a day — from the nation's airwaves, following legislation framed by Senator Jesse Helms. Ginsberg did not write this because his financial or creative future is currently threatened; he wrote in support of the process of free thought, and in solidarity with others whose livelihoods and careers are at risk. This statement is included as both an example of what an artist might say in response to efforts to censor his or her work, and as an inspiration to others, whether artists or not, to express their beliefs and support those who so desperately need it.

Statement on FCC Censorship

My poetry has been broadcast uncensored for 30 years particularly the poems *Howl*, *Sunflower Sutra*, *America*, *Kaddish*, *Kral Majales*, and *Birdbrain*. In the last two decades all these poems had been recorded on disk by Atlantic, Fantasy and Island Records, issued commercially and been broadcast by university, public, educational, and listener supported stations, such as Pacifica Network.

Most of these poems have been republished in standard anthologies used for college and high school English courses throughout America. The poem *Howl* has been translated into 24 languages, even recently into hitherto forbidden Iron Curtain countries from Poland to China.

Translations and publications into Polish, Hungarian, Czechoslovakian, Chinese, Macedonian, Serbo-Croatian, Lithuanian, and Romanian have been part and parcel of the Glasnost or freedom of speech and literature accumulated in the last half-decade in those countries. In a recent article by Bill Holm on teaching literature (including D.H. Lawrence) to students in China entitled "In China, Loving Lady Chatterley" (*New York Times Book Review*, February 18, 1990, pages 1, 30-31) we read: "Orwell's description of Big Brother's attempts to destroy and pervert sexual life is exactly and literally true. Change the names and it describes any institution like China, name your own preferred church or government." Fundamentalist mass media hucksters, Senator Jesse Helms, and the Heritage Foundation are attempting to enforce in the U.S.A. this Orwellian doublethink in destroying and perverting representation of sexual life in our art and literature.

What is their motive? Professor Holm states it precisely: "My Chinese students existed in a state of sexual suspended animation and yet underneath this mad repression, I sensed that many Chinese are hopeless romantics, doors waiting to be opened. Real sexual energy is a genuine threat to political authority. The moral Stalinists are not wrong."

I remember the insistent language of Moscow writers union bureaucrat Mr. Sagatelian at a Soviet-American literary conference in November 1985 in Vilnius just before the announcement of Glasnost. I complained of political and erotic censorship; he replied "Henry Miller will never be published in the Soviet Union."

Broadcast censorship of my poetry and the work of my peers is a direct violation of our freedom of expression. I am a citizen. I pay my taxes and I want the opinions, the political and social ideas and emotions of my art to be free from government censorship. I petition for my right to exercise liberty of speech guaranteed me by the Constitution.

I reject the insolence of self-righteous moralistic fund-raising politicians or politically ambitious priests in using my poetry as a political football for their quasi-religious agendas. I have my own agenda for emotional and intellectual and political liberty in the U.S.A. and behind the Iron Curtain. This is expressed in my poetry.

The poems named above were part of a large-scale domestic cultural and political liberalization that began with ending print and broadcast censorship of literary works 1957-1962. A series of legal trials, beginning with my poem *Howl* liberated celebrated works including books by Henry Miller, Jean Genet, D.H. Lawrence, William Burroughs, and other classic writings.

Much of my poetry is specifically aimed to rouse the sense of liberty of thought and political social expression of that thought in young adolescents. This is the very age group which the Heritage Foundation and Senator Helms's legislation and FCC regulations have attempted to prohibit me from reaching with vocal communication of my texts over the air. It is in the body, speech and mind of these young people that the state of the nation rests and I believe I am conducting spiritual war for liberation of their souls from the mass homogenization of greedy materialistic commerce and emotional desensitization. Since Walt Whitman, who foresaw this situation, many generations have suffered alienation of feeling and sympathy with their own bodies and hearts and with the bodies and hearts of all those in America and other continents that do not fit into a commercially or politically stereotyped convention of color, sex, religion, political allegiance, or personal sense of self.

Pseudo religious legal interference with my speech amounts to setting up a state religion much in the mode of an intolerant Ayatollah or a Stalinoid bureaucratic party line.

In this situation neo-conservative and religious ideologies have taken the weapons of their old communist enemies: party line, censorship, catch-22 evasion of direct responsibility for censorship, and anti-sexual politics. Their motive: to enforce the authority of their own solidified thought police religious and ethical systems. How dare I compare these self-styled patriotic citizens to communist bureaucrats? In the words of William Blake: "They became what they beheld."

These censors would abridge my rights of artistic and political freedom of speech just as communist countries did in censoring my work in 1957-1985.

Here an aesthetic consideration enters the argument. A vital characteristic of my poetry, and cause for some of its wide circulation, has been its quality of American speech, idiomatic and vernacular, a diction drawn from living language, and clarity of vocalization. The ideal is a poetry of majestic and dignified proclamation. I've tried to practice unobstructed, human voice sounded with its various rhythms & emotional tones, a poetry spoken from head, throat, and heart centers, as vocalization of sometimes inspired verse. Reading out loud has been my study and my art. This practice has affected many poets in many countries and is part of a long American tradition from the days of Whitman through William Carlos Williams's years to the lyricist Bob Dylan now. FCC censorship chills off the air my spoken broadcast of *Howl* (a critique of nuclear hypertechnology); *King of May* (a denunciation of both "communist and capitalist assholes"); *Sunflower Sutra* (panegyric to individual self-empowerment); *America* (a parody of cold-war stereotypes); *Birdbrain* — (a satire on Eastern and Western ecological stupidities); and *Kaddish* (a pouring forth of real grief and love for my late mother). How can this speech be censored from broadcast without violating our U.S. Constitution?

Censors may wish to fulminate over the word "indecency" which is never purely defined, but those who would extend Senator Helms's amendment to ban this mystific "indecency" on the air 24 hours a day cannot deny they are trying to censor art and socially relevant speech. In the case of the texts specified above, the position of the neo-conservatives is quite parallel to that of the Nazi book-burners of "degenerate works," Chinese dictators who launch attacks on "spiritual pollution," and old Stalinists forbidding erotic texts. The purpose of such censorship is to concentrate all emotional authority in the State, and eliminate all ideological and emotional competition. Conservatives proclaim their ideology to be "get the government off our backs." In this sinister comedy, I petition these so-called "neo-conservative" authoritarians to get off my back.

Walt Whitman called specifically for candor of poets and orators to follow him. Despite the unconstitutional bans that have been put on my poetry, I repeat that call for candor and affirm that I have fulfilled the Good Gray poet's prescription for a patriotic, candid, totally American art.

— ALLEN GINSBERG
1990

29

Make an Anti-Censorship Home Video Showing the Various Benefits of Free Speech in Your Community — and the Perils of Censorship

Anti-censorship videos aren't hard to make; you can rent or borrow cameras, use natural lighting, and resources from your friends, local acting companies, cable companies, and your anti-censorship group. Take advantage of the reference materials below; they'll show you how to make the best quality video you can. But what's important isn't necessarily artistic quality. What you want to present is hard-to-get information, your personal passion, and the message that the situation will worsen or improve — based on the involvement of millions of Americans.

Use the video to preach to the unconverted — invite a bunch of friends who aren't involved in the anti-censorship movement to your house and watch it; then have a group discussion on the topics it raises. Or show it as part of events put on by your anti-censorship group, local library, at your neighborhood bookstore, record shop, or video store. Once you get started, you may find that making videos is fun. Then you'll want to try to make a video about every censorship outrage that occurs in your community. Get the information to your friends and neighbors in ways that censored establishment media don't — or won't.

RESOURCES

Read articles in home video magazines, such as *Video Review*. Write them at 902 Broadway, 20th Floor, New York, NY 10011; or call (212) 477-2200. A one-year subscription is $11.97; write to P.O. Box 50148, Boulder, CO, 80321, or call (800) 525-0643.

Here is a list of home video guidebooks:

The Complete Home Video Book: A Source of Information Essential to the Video Enthusiast, by Peter Utz (Scarborough, Ontario, Canada: Prentice-Hall, 1983)

The Video Production Guide, by Lon B. McQuillin, edited by Charles Bensinger (Santa Fe, NM: Timewindow Publications, 1983)

Small Format Television Production: The Technique of Single-Camera Television Field Production, by Ronald J. Compesi and Ronald E. Sherriffs (Boston: Allyn and Bacon, 2nd ed., 1990)

Working with Video: A Comprehensive Guide to the World of Video Production, by Brian Winston (New York: AMPHOTO, 1986)

Desktop Video: A Guide to Personal and Small Business Video Production, by Austin H. Speed III (Boston: Harcourt Brace Jovanovich, 1988)

Directing Video, by Thomas Kennedy (White Plains, NY: Knowledge Industry Publications, 1988)

30
Write About Your Positive Experiences With Art

Whether for you a positive experience with art means how *Huckleberry Finn* made you understand the meaning of racism or how a heavy metal record made you understand the importance of personal freedom, write about it and get it published in your daily newspaper, arts weekly, school or union paper, or church bulletin.

Karen Hall has been a writer for the television shows "Eight is Enough," "M*A*S*H," "Hill Street Blues," and "Moonlighting." In addition, she has written the scripts for the TV movies *The Women of Brewster Place* and *Toughlove*. She writes to us about her experiences with censorship.

I know something about leading a censored life. I grew up in a small, rural Southern (predominantly Baptist) town. Everyone knew everyone; anyone who didn't share the majority opinion was ostracized. Everyone in the town had to dress the same way, vote the same way, and go to one of the three interchangeable churches.

Since most of the town was Baptist, it followed that most of my teachers were Baptists, and they had no compunction against governing our moral behavior. In the seventh grade, I had one particularly fierce teacher, Mrs. Clemments, a 75-year-old redhead who had just said no to mandatory retirement. Every Monday morning, Mrs. Clemments would ask to see the hands of those who had gone to church on Sunday. Then she would ask to see the hands of those who had gone to a Baptist church. The Baptists would get As, the lesser church-goers would get Bs, and those who slept in on Sunday mornings and were foolish enough to admit it were left at the mercy of their penmanship.

Mrs. Clemments would routinely inspect purses to see what non-Christian propaganda her female students might be carting around. One morning, she opened my purse and found a page torn from *Family Circle* magazine. I was saving a form to order a $9.95 print of Man O'War, the legendary racehorse with whom I was obsessed at the time. On the other side of the page there was an ad for soap, which featured the backside of a naked woman. When Mrs. Clemments saw this, she hauled me up to the front of the class and held the picture up for everyone to see. She read me the riot act about a woman's body being a beautiful thing and not something to be treated like a dirty joke. My classmates quickly leapt to the only logical conclusion — that I was gay — and treated me accordingly for almost three years. I had never even known the picture was there.

So I have known since childhood that when the self-appointed morally superior start dictating standards for the rest of us, we end up at the mercy of their bizarre subjectivity. These arbitrary decisions are not harmless. Like a radioactive cloud, they spread over us and damage us in ways we don't even see until it's too late.

I have since fled 3,000 miles from my hometown, but I have not managed to escape this cloud. Instead, I find myself viewing it from a different angle. For the past 10 years I have made my living as a television writer and producer, which allows me daily contact with the forces that are playing "Mrs. Clemments" for the entire country. The chain of censorship goes like this: Network Broadcast Standards (a.k.a. censors) react to sponsors who react to pressure groups and religious fanatics. Viewers hear about the more publicized cases, but they don't begin to know the extent to which what they see is controlled by this system.

The people who work for each network's broadcast standards department are there to protect the network from any trouble, negative publicity or, worst of all, sponsor boycotts. They have to be mindful of the views of a wide range of crusaders, but they themselves are not necessarily upstanding church-goers. In a meeting on one of my recent projects, the head of broadcast standards for one of the major networks informed me that he didn't "give a fuck" about quality, and for the next hour he continued to use language that would make Luther Campbell blush. But he protected America from "50 percent of the damns and hells" I had used in my script.

In 1985 I wrote a TV movie called *Toughlove*. It was well-received, ranking number 10 for the week it aired. It also won the Scott Newman Drug Abuse Prevention Award. But two weeks before it went into production, ABC Broadcast Standards tried to keep it from being made. They did not want us to make a movie that depicted teenagers using drugs. Their five-page list of specific objections was mind-boggling. My favorite item was the one that said we couldn't show a coke vial with a spoon in the top because teenagers might be enticed into drug abuse by being educated about the "cute paraphernalia" that was available. We pointed out that this would not be new information to most teenagers, and that perhaps the ones who weren't already doing drugs were not refraining because they thought the accompanying equipment wasn't cute enough.

The *Toughlove* scenario is just a representative example of a problem that is pervasive and growing worse. I was especially sickened by Burger King's recent ad announcing its dedication to television that supports "traditional family values" — evidently a result of pressure from Rev. Donald Wildmon's CLeaR-TV. Whenever someone gets on the soapbox about "good old-fashioned American values," I wonder what they mean. Old-fashioned values like corporal punishment? Second-class citizenship for women, children, and all minorities? All the various soul-murdering techniques that have landed 15 million Americans in detox programs? Yeah, let's definitely get back to those.

I do agree that a boycott of Burger King is in order, though, for its lily-livered kowtowing. This destructive precedent is bound to come back to haunt television's creative community. I hope all the people who think this threat is meaningless will be content to live without shows like "Hill Street Blues," "M*A*S*H" (which was always on the Moral Majority's hit list because of its "liberal, anti-war" stance), "Thirty-something," and "L.A. Law." Shows like these are becoming harder to sell every day. The shows that manage to survive the current fear-based programming strategy will make "Mr. Belvedere" look adventuresome. At least no one will have to worry about thinking or learning anything.

But my career is no longer the primary motivation for my politics. I now have a much more important reason to fight censorship — my 15-month-old daughter. Granted, her presence muddies the waters, since there are a lot of things in the world that I am not particularly looking forward to her being exposed to. But I have been exposed, in one way or another, to most of what's out there, and I have managed to survive corruption. I want Juli, at appropriate ages, to see the full scope of life. I trust her to sort through it all and find her own moral code, and I don't want her to have to fight for that right the way I had to. I don't want her to choose the "right" thing out of fear, and I *certainly* don't want her to be forced or legislated into adhering to someone else's standards.

As a writer, I am going to continue to rail against those who ask me to espouse the moral rantings of a few power-crazed evangelists and the sheep who follow them. As a parent, I am going to do anything in my power to keep the "Mrs. Clemments" of the world from looking into purses and shaming anyone with whom they disagree.

I led a censored life for 23 years. I am currently spending a fortune in therapy trying to figure out who the hell I am, because I was never given a chance to know. You can't know who you are if you don't know what you believe, and you can't know what you believe when it is being dictated to you. This is the legacy our children face if we allow a bunch of Calvinistic kooks to tell them what they can see, what they can listen to, what they can like. I know a lot about where that lands you, and I wouldn't wish it on my worst enemy.

31
Become a Voter Registrar; Organize a Voter Registration Drive

"The United States is the only major democracy where government assumes no responsibility for helping citizens cope with voter registration procedures . . ."
— Frances Fox Piven and Richard A. Cloward
Why Americans Don't Vote (New York: Random House, 1989).

Bring others into the political process by helping to register voters. Americans are constantly accused of not being interested in politics. Indeed, in many areas, it's common for less than half the eligible citizens to vote. Ronald Reagan's 1984 "landslide" was accomplished by attracting *less than 25 percent* of the eligible voters! In that election, more Americans sat it out than voted for *any* candidate.

The real reason Americans don't vote isn't apathy. The political machine has systematically excluded citizens from participating in the electoral process. Voter registration in the United States is far more complicated and mysterious than it needs to be — certainly, far more complex and mystifying than in any European nation.

If how to become a voter is a mystery to most Americans, how to register others to vote must seem like one of the secrets of the universe. But not everywhere: In fact, in some California communities, for example, voter registrars are actually paid — 50 cents to a dollar per person registered. And, as Piven and Cloward point out, more Americans *will* vote — if we can reach them. And, if polls and surveys are to be believed, most of those Americans will favor First Amendment freedoms far more than the minority that now controls our political process.

If You Want to Become a Voter Registrar

To set the wheels in motion, get in touch with your local voter registrar and ask to be deputized. If you don't know the procedure in your area, call your state's board of elections at the phone number listed in #2, and ask.

If you want to become a voter registrar and conduct a drive, you're protected by the First Amendment and the Voting Rights Act. If you live in an area where elected officials represent a minority that would lose control if more voters became active, you may need every bit of that protection. Official registrars can not only be unsympathetic but actively hostile. Consult an attorney if you are harassed.

Form a voter registration group: More than one person can become a registrar, and you'll be better able to solve problems collectively. You'll also register more voters. One group that may help, at least by providing information, is Rock The Vote!, which was organized by influential members of the music industry in the wake of censorship attacks. Contact RTV at P.O. Box 5434, Beverly Hills, CA 90209; (213) 276-8364.

You should target areas that have had historically low turnouts. These communities are traditionally neglected by the political process, and are disenfranchised. But in many instances, these are exactly the people most eager to vote, if only someone will show them how. The most experienced and successful group working with poor and minority voters is Project Vote. They've published *How to Develop a Voter Registration Plan* and *How to Register Voters at a Central Site*, as well as general information, flyers, and training videos. Contact Project Vote at: 1424 16th Street, NW, Suite 101, Washington, DC 20036; (202) 328-1500.

Once you have your voter registrar credentials and equipment, set up shop at a convenient location such as a busy street corner, in a park, outside a shopping center, or outside a local school. (Almost any place on a college campus can be effective.) Make sure you're available at hours when people have time to stop and fill out the forms — often that means weekends and evening hours are the best times. If you're registering people in a community where English is not the primary language, try to provide bilingual registration forms.

Be creative and assertive (not obnoxious). Remind passers-by that they have nothing to lose by voting, and may have a lot to gain. Make up signs, wear costumes, shout out slogans — entice people into signing up.

Follow-up is also important: Try to keep a record of all those you register so your group can follow up, making sure people get to the polls on Election Day. Or work with a group such as Project Vote, which not only registers voters, but which also conducts "Get Out the Vote" drives. Ask local celebrities to do public service announcements, which can be cheaply recorded and then broadcast for free on radio, local TV, and community access cable.

32
Form a Group That Establishes a First Amendment Litmus Test for Politicians

Make sure that the politicians know that you *will* vote on the basis of their support of free speech and opposition to censors, no matter how well-connected the censors might be. Organize campaigns to defeat pols who prosecute censorship cases and to support candidates who make specific programs to support free speech and the arts part of their platforms. These can have real impact: Artists for Washington was a significant factor in Harold Washington's mayoral victories in Chicago.

• Another group that has been effective in local elections is the San Francisco Arts Democratic Club. Contact them for advice on what your local group can do: P.O. Box 460524-94146, San Francisco, CA 94146; (415) 995-ARTS.

• Contact the Center for Arts Advocacy, c/o Arts Partners, 861 West Wrightwood, Chicago, IL 60614, (312) 472-2124, for information on how arts communities across the country have worked in elections and city politics. If you have experiences to share, send them to the Center.

• Find out who your local arts organizations are and form a coalition with

them to screen candidates. Make each candidate say specifically what he or she will do to ensure the rights of artists and the press, and how they will respond to other First Amendment issues. Perhaps your coalition can also form and fund an Arts PAC (political action committee). After all, arts funding depends on having elected officials who will serve this constituency.

• Put already elected officials — city councilmembers, mayors, legislators, governors — on the spot by asking them to declare a week honoring the First Amendment. This doesn't mean a holiday; it means a week when teachers will introduce First Amendment discussions in their classrooms, when civic groups around the state or city will talk about free speech issues, when attention can be focused on the issue in a variety of ways.

The state of Ohio and the city of St. Louis, Missouri, issued such declarations in honor of Banned Books Week, for the purpose of "informing our citizens as to the nature and magnitude of the threat censorship poses to our First Amendment rights of freedom of speech and press, the cornerstone of American liberty."

33
Start an Anti-Censorship Petition Campaign

An anti-censorship petition can be addressed to anybody — from a non-government censor to a local city council or sheriff to the President of the United States. It's probably best to operate on the same basis as the problem: If you're dealing with cops contemptuous of free speech, address the petition locally; if you want to tackle Jesse Helms, go state-wide if you live in North Carolina, nationwide otherwise.

This is a great way to send a message to politicians, police, and other officials. You write a basic message opposing whatever infractions of free speech have been committed, get others to endorse it with their signatures and addresses, and send it to the relevant authorities. A petition sends a very distinct message about the public's concern with censorship, it signals that people are annoyed enough to do something (it's a little like voting — a point not lost on elected officials), and, best of all, it builds a core list of First Amendment supporters, with names and addresses.

When you have a sufficient number of signatures, present the petitions to the persons or organizations to whom they're addressed, and call a press conference to announce what you're doing. If the addressee won't accept the petitions, so much the better: Have a big pile of 'em with you at the press event, so that folks can see what the censors are missing. (If the censor does accept the petitions, present them *after* the press conference, so that you can still have that big pile as a prop.) You'll also want to have as many well-known supporters on hand as you possibly can — if there are musicians, writers, or artists involved in your campaign, attendance at this event is a must. (That doesn't mean some-body's a rat if they have a schedule conflict and can't make it; it means you'll try to schedule the event to take advantage of their availability.)

How many petitions or signatures does it take to make an impact? The original Moral Majority petitions, which caused such a splash and kicked off the censors' feeding frenzy of the '80s, had only 50,000 signatures; that's out of a total United States population of *250 million*. And presenting 50,000 signatures to the U.S. Justice Department in 1989 got considerable media coverage for the rock anti-censorship group Music in Action. Again, that was a national campaign. On a local basis, far smaller numbers can have a great impact: In a town of 100,000, a thousand signatures would send a very, very big message.

34
Boycott Products Made and Marketed by Companies That Fund the Censors

Boycotts are very effective ways of making companies take notice. A 1989 *Business Week* poll showed that 76 percent of Americans are willing to boycott a corporation if it does harm to society. Broadcasters, for instance, often say that they won't air controversial material because they believe that consumers will be turned off to their sponsors and avoid the products the shows are selling. Such pressure shouldn't only keep material *off* the air. If anti-censorship activists use boycotts to attack the policies of such companies, it becomes a reason for keeping free speech alive.

The simplest way (there is no "easy" way) to find out which companies support censorship is to see which companies have made campaign contributions to avid politico-censors like Senator Helms and Congressman Dana Rohrbacher. Campaign records are — perhaps deliberately — available only in haphazard condition, with no logically organized arrangement of names, dates, or places. Additionally, they're often available only on microfiche, which usually means you have to hand-copy the relevant parts, so there's a lot of elbow grease involved; but the potential payoff makes it worthwhile.

After you've learned which companies you're going to target, go to the library and find a copy of the firm's annual report, or contact a stockbroker, who can usually get one to you in a couple of days. Annuals list the names and positions of the company's outside directors, usually on the back. In addition to those who are officers of other corporations, you'll often find that these outside directors are university presidents, media celebrities, and public officials. Contact them by letter, phone, or fax, and ask why they're allowing the firm to support censorship. As directors, they're responsible for all its activities. If they don't or won't take steps to reverse the censorship-support policy, boycott their companies too, or picket the institutions that they represent. (Again, before forming a picket line, see an attorney to learn the procedure.)

35
Start a Grassroots Anti-Censorship Organization

Using the principle "Think globally — Act locally," start a grassroots anti-censorship group and see it mushroom into an organization with national impact. Or, if there's already one in your area, join it and support it.

National anti-censorship groups can often give you helpful advice on how to start your own group. Or contact these already formed local anti-censorship coalitions for advice on starting yours.

Washington Coalition Against Censorship, 5503 17th Street NW, #640, Seattle, WA 98107, (206) 884-6418

Delaware Valley Anti-Censorship Coalition, c/o Messick, P.O. Box 8992, Newark, DE 19714, (302) 731-5478

Chicago Artists' Coalition/Committee for Artists' Rights, 5 West Grand, Chicago, IL 60610, (312) 670-2060

Parents for Rock and Rap (PFRR), c/o Mary Morello, Box 53, Libertyville, IL 60048

Mary Morello of PFRR has the following advice:

GETTING OFF THE GROUND

1. When you have a cause as basic as the First Amendment to the Constitution, you have a great percentage of the population on your side.
2. Know what your goals are, and what you advocate.
3. Announce through the news media that you have an organization: Give its name, what it stands for, and the membership requirements.

MONEY

It may take a little initial cash on your part. PFRR started with $208 plus a $100 donation from an established anti-censorship organization. A great deal of money is not essential: Paper, envelopes, stamps, and phone call costs are minimal. In PFRR's original pitch, the organization asked for a $3 membership fee; the money did come in and the group is still in the black.

GET TO WORK

Along the road, you have to research the censors so that you know what you're up against. Perhaps question why the less powerful and grassroots artists and audiences are going after the censors, while no one hears from record company boards of directors or museum boards of directors.

Parents for Rock and Rap's original goal was to create a center where members could send in information on censorship in the music industry. The center would then reach all members for response. It now has 17 regional representatives to handle the members in 36 states and Nova Scotia, Canada. In six months, over 360 letters came in.

By November 1990, only a few months after its founding, PFRR had sent out two different packets to the group representatives. In turn, they reproduced the materials and sent it on to the members.

The packets not only contain information but also contain suggestions for specific things to do in order to combat censorship, membership applications to recruit more members, lists of addresses of pro- and anti-censorship groups, and any additional information that would be valuable. Members may act individually, work with their regional rep, or under the guidance of the center in Libertyville. Some members are affiliated with other anti-censorship groups.

36
Start an
Anti-Censorship Newsletter

An anti-censorship newsletter is very cheap to do — you should be able to get 500 copies of a four-page newsletter printed for less than $100. A few donations and/or subscriptions will cover your costs. (Your list of subscribers also becomes a great tool for other mailings and organizing efforts.) Talk to local photographers about taking pictures for your newsletter; this won't raise the cost much. Approach local printers or ad agencies to see if they'll produce your newsletter on their desktop publishing system, for free. Or perhaps your union, school, or church has such equipment available. Computer-created newsletters look much more attractive and rapidly increase readership, and that makes them much more effective.

You can usually find at least a few samples of newsletters on other topics — finance, etc. — at your local library. They'll give you an idea of the options on format, size, price, and other details.

To get some ideas, you can write:

The *Newsletter on Intellectual Freedom*, East Huron Street, Chicago, IL 60611; (312) 944-6780. A bimonthly publication of the American Library Association that reports on censorship incidents across the U.S., summarizes recent First Amendment court cases, and offers a bibliography. (Subscription: $25 per year.)

Rock & Roll Confidential, P.O. Box 341305, Los Angeles, CA 90034. A newsletter devoted largely to opposing music censorship edited by Dave Marsh, author of this book. (Subscription: $24 per year.)

Rock Out Censorship, c/o John Woods, 320 South Cadiz Street, Jewett, OH 43986; (614) 946-4685. A local version of the *Rock & Roll Confidential* idea, ROC describes itself as "dedicated to the fight against all forms of censorship. Supports the struggle for FREEDOM OF EXPRESSION and FREEDOM OF SPEECH, be it in music, art, literature, or film." (Subscription to ROC's bimonthly newsletter, *The ROC*, is $6 per year; $20 gets you a subscription, a T-shirt asking, "Who Made Tipper Gore God?" and all updates. Send T-shirt size.)

Tips on Printers

The ALA's *Banned Books Week '90: A Resource Guide* offers the following advice on finding and using printers. There are essentially two kinds of printers — instant printers and commercial printers. Instant printers, usually able to do a job in a few days, are best used for small, simple jobs. If your order is very large, it may be more economical to use a commercial printer, even though their process is slower. To find a good one, ask local businesses or arts groups in your area. Call the commercial printers recommended and speak to a sales representative. Some points to keep in mind:

1. If you're using instant printers ask them to use a metal plate. This costs more than a plastic plate but will result in a better product.

2. Ask to see paper samples; to save money, use what's in stock.

3. Show the printer a comparable finished piece to make sure both of you understand the type and quality you're looking for.

Recruit your local printer or print shop. These businesses frequently come under attack for printing things censors don't like. And let people know about printers who censor, who refuse to print things that they disagree with, or that they fear will cost them business. Remember — the latter issue cuts both ways! Printers who support the First Amendment deserve to get the business of your local anti-censorship organization and other arts groups.

37
Contact Local Arts and Educational Groups; Persuade Them to Stage a Free Speech Event

Contact your local museum, art gallery, music club, bookstore, library, school, etc., and offer to help them organize a "Free Speech" event. Most arts organizations, museums, and libraries — even, or especially, the most censorship-beleaguered — are understaffed and/or on a very tight budget. Many clubs are strapped by the strictures of the bottom line. There are lots of challenging programs they could present, and lots of worthwhile events they could stage, if there were only time and money. Above all, they need to see a clear demand for these events and a body of volunteers willing to provide both ideas and, best of all, people power.

Once you find an organization willing to put on an event staffed by volunteers, see if you can get them to absorb advertising costs. As a trade-off, you and your crew can stick up posters and pass out leaflets announcing what you're up to.

There are innumerable possibilities for such events: Do you want to do an intensely educational program on the history of censorship versus free art, music, and cinema in America? Or would you prefer to present the writing, art, or performance of a censored or banned artist? Perhaps you can rally a roster of local bands, to protest against record labeling or the local sheriff department's prejudice against rap and heavy metal. Perhaps you and a group of teachers from your school (or your child's school) can coordinate an assembly or a historical presentation about censorship or some related topic. (These used to be called "teach-ins.")

Whatever you decide to do, certainly your local museum or gallery can suggest contacts and provide a fertile Rolodex from which you can network. Once you begin organizing, you'll be surprised by how many other groups are willing to organize or participate.

RESOURCES

Experience Counts. To find out how some others have already put together such programs and events, contact:

BAUhaus Arts Center, 1713 North Charles Street, Baltimore, MD 21230; (301) 659-5443. The BAUhaus has an ongoing exhibition of censored artworks, and has shown the work of over 260 artists since it opened in the spring of 1990.

Booksellers for Social Responsibility, c/o Guild Books, 2456 North Lincoln Avenue, Chicago, IL 60614; (312) 525-3667. This national organization of bookstores has not only sponsored numerous events around book censorship, it has also sponsored activities in its member stores that have put the spotlight on *real* obscenities, such as homelessness and lack of health care. Write or call Guild Books to find out which member store is nearest you.

Central Park SummerStage, 830 Fifth Avenue, New York, NY 10021; (212) 360-2777. This is a multi-cultural arts series that presents everything from modern dance to rap, from spoken word to world music, to an audience of approximately 300,000 people per year. SummerStage included a historical look at censorship in its 1990 "Talking Book Series." Carl Bernstein and Eliot Asinof, two writers whose lives were adversely affected by the blacklists of the McCarthy era, read from their works and held a question and answer session on "Censors: Then and Now," among other topics.

Chap's on Main, 105 East Michigan Avenue, Kalamazoo, MI 49007; (616) 393-3922. Chap's is a rock and roll club that has staged anti-censorship concerts. These have not only raised money, but they also spawned an organization, FACT (Fans Against the Censorship Threat), with its own newsletter. Contact: Paul Toth.

The Greater Kansas City Coalition Against Censorship, 106 East 31st Terrace, Kansas City, MO 64111; (816) 421-4449. The Coalition played a leading role in organizing "Culture Under Fire," a highly successful week-long series of performances, workshops, and presentations that brought together a cross-section of Midwestern artists, writers, and musicians, helping them get to know each other and make plans to fight censorship.

Real Art Ways, 56 Arbor Street, Hartford, CT 06106; (203) 233-1006. This center for new and experimental arts presented, over the course of its 1990-91 season, John Fleck, Karen Finley, Holly Hughes, and Tim Miller, the four performance artists who were denied grants by NEA chairman John Frohnmayer (despite two successive unanimous recommendations from the NEA Peer Panel). Executive director Will K. Wilkins said: "I would never have programmed all four of these artists simply because of the NEA decision; it's not as clear-cut as that, it's an issue of gay rights and civil liberties. These people were singled out because of their take on sexuality, because of their embodiment of it." Wilkins and his staff also arranged fund-raising tie-ins with each of these four artists, in order to support lesser-known and equally controversial performance artists.

38
Set a Good Example — Start a Parents Group to Combat Censorship

Set a good example for your kids. Start a parents group to protect your children from censorship. This group can advance a positive free speech agenda, support progressive teachers and administrators, and educate kids about the First Amendment and the value of active good citizenship. Invite sympathetic teachers to join your group.

Sponsor an anti-censorship discussion group in your community —your library or school would be a good place for such a forum. This will give students, parents, teachers, and others a chance to talk about works of art that some find troublesome, and others find enlightening. Not wanting to censor something doesn't mean endorsing it, and such a forum can be a chance to hear many different points of view, some of which will surprise even the organizers.

39
Contact Local TV Stations and Propose a "Censored Films Festival"

Contact your local television station — public, commercial, or cable access — and propose that it show a "Censored Films Festival." This could include historic and popular films, such as *The Birth of a Nation*,

The Exorcist, *The Last Temptation of Christ*, and *Carnal Knowledge*, which all faced challenges from censorship forces. Also include films about censorship issues, such as Francois Truffaut's *Fahrenheit 451*; *Storm Center*, starring Bette Davis; either version of *1984*; *The Seven Minutes*; and *Inherit the Wind*, starring Spencer Tracy.

The films of John Waters are good candidates for any censored films festival. Waters has directed *Hair Spray*, *Pink Flamingos*, *Cry Baby*, and many other films, all of them motivated by an extreme hatred of censors and their values. Many censors have responded in kind. Most recently, *Pink Flamingos* was charged with obscenity in Orlando, Florida. His experiences inspired him to write and publish the following.

An Open Letter to the Censors

Dear Mr. and Mrs. Censor,

Just a short note to thank you for all the extra profits you've helped me to make on the writing, producing, and directing of my so-called "obscene" films. Money couldn't buy all the free publicity and notoriety you've given me over the years. Since everyone knows that as soon as you tell somebody they can't see a movie, they run directly towards the theater and pull out their wallet, you've been my favorite press agents to date. Keep calling me every name in the book, even put me under arrest — just don't forget to spell the movie's title correctly so I can cash in on your welcome condemnation. Of course, if you *really* wanted to censor something, all you would have to do is ignore it and nobody would care about it. But then *you* wouldn't get your name in the paper and we couldn't have that, could we? I guess we all have our own scrapbooks to fill. See you in hell.

John Waters

You can also do this project with your local movie revival house or campus film society. Plan the program using *Banned Films: Movies, Censors and the First Amendment* by Edward de Grazia and Roger K. Newman (New York: R.R. Bowker, 1982). Also, contact the American Library Association, 50 East Huron Street, Chicago, IL 60611, (312) 944-6780, to rent a copy of its 16mm anti-censorship film, *The Speaker*, which depicts a high school committee fighting censorship.

40
Use Community Access Cable TV or Community Radio to Raise Awareness of Free Speech Issues

Use local nonprofit radio stations (which may be associated with a university or operate independently, depending on public donations rather than commercials for revenue) or "community access" channels of your cable system as forums to expose censorship and to rally artists and free speech supporters.

Call the radio stations, and ask for the program director's office. The staff should be able to give you information on how to submit a community programming proposal. Think through your show before taping it or broadcasting it live. If you're just playing music and talking, make sure you have your records ready; dead air is dreadful. If you're running a panel discussion, make sure that everybody has a chance to quickly get acquainted before the show begins, and that there are clear ground rules for the conversation. If you're going to take live phone calls, make sure to screen them before putting them on the air. Work at the radio station if you can, since it almost inevitably has superior equipment and other facilities.

At some cable TV community access stations you have to pay a fee to use the equipment, but often, you don't. Round up some friends with technical experience (a little counts for a lot) to actually do the camera work.

Whether you're doing TV or radio, make sure you keep a tape of all live broadcasts. There are at least three benefits to this: You can learn from your mistakes, by seeing or hearing them played back. You can use the tape over and over again, as a rerun on the same station, on other nearby stations, or at free speech meetings and anti-censorship recruiting sessions. Finally, you'll have protected yourself by making a record of what you really said, in case somebody tries to distort it.

Here are some other things you can do with your local stations to combat radio censorship:

• Contact music and programming directors and ask them to join the fight against censorship through special programming aimed at informing listeners about the problem. "Fairness" demands that views from both sides be aired and that the station remain officially neutral — but allowing free speech advocates equal time is essential, since telling the truth often carries the argument.

• Remember, the FCC must respond to *all* complaints, not just those it finds congenial. When you hear a broadcaster censor material by editing or omitting parts, or supporting or endorsing censorship, write letters of complaint to the Federal Communications Commission, Complaints and Investigations Bureau Chief, Enforcement Division, Mass Media Bureau, at 1919 M Street, NW, Washington, DC 20554.

• If major radio stations won't play your music, contact Zoom Black Magic, the only unlicensed radio network in the country. Write them at 8 Kaviland Street, Fresno, CA 93706 or 333 North 12 Street, Springfield, IL 62702.

RESOURCES

"Censorship or Selection: Choosing Books for Public Schools." An hour-long video-tape from Columbia University's esteemed journalism school, shows a 22-member panel responding to the issues of how books get into classrooms and libraries —and how they're sometimes removed. Create your own program, or get your local TV station to show this one. $150 from Media and Society Seminars, Graduate School of Journalism, Columbia University, New York, NY 10027.

The Video Source Book, edited by David Wiener (Detroit, MI: Gale Research, $210 — get your butt to the library for this one) is updated yearly. Its sixth edition listed 40,000 programs available from more than 800 sources, and featured seven anti-censorship videos: "Bags", "Books Under Fire", "Censorship in a Free Society", "Censorship or Selection: Choosing Books for Public Schools", "Free Press, Fair Trial", "Inside the Anonymous Source", "What Johnny Can't Read." The book gives the complete ordering information, program description, release date, and other information for each tape.

Other useful books on cable and community access include:

The Barefoot Channel: Community Television as a Tool for Social Change, by Kim Goldberg (Vancouver: New Star Books, 1990)

Cable Television and the First Amendment, by Patrick Parsons (Lexington, Mass.: Health and Co., 1987)

Cable Television: A Reference Guide to Information, by Ronald Garay (New York: Greenwood Press, 1988)

Variety Sourcebook, compiled by Marilyn J. Matelski and David O. Thomas (Boston: Focal Press, 1990)

Producer's Sourcebook, available from the National Cable Television Association, 1724 Massachusetts Avenue, NW, Washington, DC 20036, (202) 775-3550

41
Create a Public Service Announcement to Be Aired Over the Radio

Create a public service announcement to run on your local radio station. For ideas and guidelines contact the American Library Association, 50 East Huron Street, Chicago, IL 60611, (312) 944-6780, for a copy of its *Banned Books Week '90: A Resource Book* ($20), which contains sample radio spots. Or contact a local advertising agency — or individuals who work at one — and get them to work with you on a *pro bono* (free) basis. You can also create ads for TV or newspaper and magazine use. Make sure these are Public Service Announcements, devoted to freedom of speech and as non-partisan as possible — that way, they should run for free. Remember, all media run *some* public service announcements and all of them have a stake in the continued support of the First Amendment. (Don't be surprised if some of them need to be reminded of those facts, though.)

42
Stage a Mock Trial on Censorship

Stage a mock trial or moot court on First Amendment rights. Get a local law school — or maybe a stage troupe or drama class — to participate. Put a banned book or record on trial. Or try to prevent a speaker from appearing. It'll give you a chance to adopt outrageous positions and take an inexpensive look at the frustrations and limitations of fighting censorship in the court system.

RESOURCES

Mock court materials, and other valuable information, are available from:

The Constitutional Rights Foundation, 601 South Kingsley Drive, Los Angeles, CA 90005; (213) 487-5590. Their mock-trial packets include instructor's guides and judge's instructions on a different topic each year.

The National Institute for Citizen Education in the Law, Street Law Program, 711 G Street, SE, Washington, DC 20003; (202) 546-6644. Publishes an annual mock-trial packet with three different cases.

The Center for Civic Education, 5146 North Douglas Fir Road, Calabasas, CA 91302; (818) 340-9320. Develops curriculum materials to teach high school students about the Constitution.

The American Bar Association, 750 North Lake Shore Drive, Chicago, IL 60611; (312) 988-5000. Publishes *Speaking and Writing the Truth: Community Forums on the First Amendment* by Robert S. Peck and Mary Mannemann — $4.95 from Order Fulfillment, (312) 846-0004 — which contains detailed instructions for debates, town hall meetings, mock trials, and mock legislative hearings.

43
Make Sure Local Schools Have a Course on Freedom of Speech

Contact your area high school, university, or community college and make sure it has a course on freedom of speech. If not, help them develop one. Maybe even volunteer to teach it.

Danny Alexander and David Cantwell, publishers of *A Sign of the Times*, also teach a free speech course at Johnson County (Kansas) Community College. They write:

STUDENTS

If you're a college student, many schools offer continuing education programs that allow people from the community to teach courses on issues outside the standard college curriculum. If you don't feel qualified to lead a class, try convincing sympathetic teachers (they don't have to be experts) to explore making one happen. If your instructors seem hesitant, tell them you'll volunteer some time to help alleviate their course overload. If they argue that they need to see what the administration thinks of the idea, offer to attend a meeting with them. Often, an enthusiastic student can work wonders in motivating a teacher. And, regardless of discipline, all instructors have a vested interest in freedom of speech, and most of them know it.

You can also bring up the idea of free speech in your junior high, high school, or college class, whenever it's appropriate. For example, if your class is discussing *The Catcher in the Rye*, ask: "Isn't this on the American Library Association's list of banned books?" Then ask why. If the rest of the class doesn't get your point, ask: "Isn't this just like what happened to 2 Live Crew?"

Allan Bloom's *The Closing of the American Mind: How Higher Education Has Failed Democracy and Impoverished the Souls of Today's Students* goes to great pains to lay American academic troubles at pop culture's doorstep. But an educational system that attempts to create enlightened citizens while consciously ignoring most of the world which students will encounter once their schooling is over is the real failure of democracy, the true soul impoverishment.

Make connections between the things you're studying in art, English, history (or whatever else), and the rock music you listen to and the TV you watch. If your teacher resists making such connections, don't stop. Reinforce your argument with every example that applies. At some point, no matter what your teacher's preference, the validity of the issues you care about will become undeniable.

TEACHERS

Beyond suggesting new free speech–related courses to their administrations, teachers can also incorporate First Amendment activities into any class they are currently teaching. Discussion of censorship is relevant to any topic, from physical science to art history. (Galileo's persecution for rejecting the geocentric universe and the 19th century's violent reaction to Impressionism are just two examples.) Present the facts and let your students make the connections with today's events.

Instructors have had great success encouraging such discussions, using Madonna and the Simpsons (among others) as catalysts to liven up the classroom. These are the teachers who bridge the gap between their curriculum and the lives of their students.

But the arbitrary barriers that separate "high" culture (deemed appropriate for study) from "low" culture (the stuff everyone really uses and enjoys) are entrenched in our current educational system. Only a handful of colleges — including Bowling Green (Ohio) State University's pioneering program — offer courses dealing with popular culture studies, and even fewer offer such a curriculum without condescension.

Strategies for developing a First Amendment course and the use of free-speech learning strategies are limitless because the topic shifts with the context. Fortunately, with education's burgeoning writing-across-the-curriculum movement, critical thinking and writing skills are becoming increasingly emphasized in progressive classrooms all across America. Teaching that forces students to make connections and think for themselves is the wave of the future. What more appropriate way to catch that wave than with discussions of students' freedom of speech?

RESOURCES

Censorship and Selection: Issues and Answers for Schools, by Henry F. Reichman. Shows how to develop viable policies ranging from how to handle censorship complaints to how to select learning materials. Specific recommendations on how schools and libraries can plan for potential crises are also available. $12.95 from American Library Association, 50 East Huron Street, Chicago, IL 60611; (312) 944-6780.

44
Contact Others Concerned About Censorship — Put It in the Want Ads!

If you have a local weekly paper that concentrates on music and pop culture, place a classified ad asking other fans concerned about censorship to get in touch with you. Get acquainted so you can mobilize when you need to. You might also want to consider taking out classifieds to locate your local "Nielsen families" — those whose TV sets are monitored by the network ratings service, A.C. Nielsen Co. Make sure that they know the issues, and that they *report* watching censored programs like "The Simpsons."

WARNING: The Nielsen Co. won't like you doing this very much — they're afraid you'll "taint" their results — and asking Nielsen families to get in touch will confuse the hell out of people actually *named* Nielsen. But such ads get results.

45
Talk to Teachers About What They're Doing to Ensure Free Speech

Contact your state and local teacher's union, your university's faculty senate, or the university's branch of the American Association of University Professors (AAUP) and ask what they're doing to ensure free speech in the classroom. Teachers are often hired and/or fired on ideological or even theological grounds; ask how you can support teachers' freedom of speech, and follow through.

Points to Keep in Mind

• Accuracy in Academia, a right-wing group that monitors lectures and targets professors they find too liberal, attacked an Arizona State University professor for spending "excessive" time on the dangers of nuclear war in his political science group. AIA presumably believes he should have given equal time to the pleasures of such wars.

• Teaching about evolution, the backbone of the biological sciences, is compromised in many textbooks and curricula because of pressures from "scientific creationists," who contend that the Biblical account of the origins of life on Earth is literally true. Censors such as the American Family Association and Focus on the Family are among the leading creationist propagandists.

• The U.S. government now limits the distribution of *un*classified information so severely that the essential discussion and exchange of scientific information has been seriously impaired.

RESOURCES

The Center for Civic Education, 5146 North Douglas Fir Road, Calabasas, CA

91302; (818) 340-9320. Develops curriculum materials to teach high school students about the Constitution.

Censorship and Selection: Issues and Answers for Schools, by Henry F. Reichman. Shows how to develop viable policies ranging from how to handle censorship complaints to how to select learning materials. Specific recommendations on how schools and libraries can plan for potential crises are also available. The book costs $12.95 and is available from American Library Association, 50 East Huron Street, Chicago, IL 60611; (312) 944-6780.

46
Picket the Censors

Picket the censors. If there's a church trying to enforce its morality on your whole community, maybe its membership needs to have some visible evidence of how others feel. If school board members are pushing censorship in the classroom, they should know how many people disagree with them. If cops are on a crusade, they should be told that many people in the community think that they should mind their own business.

The peaceful picketing of places of business and the domiciles of public figures, such as censors, is an important part of free speech. However, it's also legally tricky, and various local ordinances and police attitudes may determine what happens when you do it. Contact the most experienced civil liberties attorney you can find to learn the facts about your area. If the local police don't obey the law, take the bust nonviolently and then SUE. (Picketing is not, however, recommended as a fund-raiser.)

47
Sue the Bastards!

If you can't convince the censors to back off, you may be able to *force* them off. How? Sue!

For the anti-censorship movement to completely succeed, the uncommitted need to be moved to action and the hearts and minds of the censors themselves must be won over. The uncommitted can be moved. But the devotion of censors to various hidden agendas makes it unlikely they'll ever admit their error, much less move to correct it. You may *have* to sue.

Ben Eicher, an attorney in Rapid City, South Dakota, writes:

> Whether you work through the American Civil Liberties Union (ACLU — see #19) or otherwise, anti-censorship litigation only gets to court if there are people willing to start lawsuits and lawyers willing to litigate. If your constitutionally protected rights have been violated — as an artist, a speaker, a demonstrator, or even as a consumer/audience member —*you* may be entitled to start your own civil liberties case.

CHOOSING A LAWYER

Because cases involving constitutional rights tend to be unique, finding a lawyer specializing in First Amendment law is important.

Contact your local or state bar association or the local ACLU. Find out which lawyers in your vicinity are known to accept civil liberties cases. Another option is to go to your local library or to any local attorney's office and ask to see the *Martindale-Hubbell Bar Register*, an encyclopedia of attorneys, for your area. This is a multi-volume reference that includes the name and area of practice of almost any reputable lawyer. If you end up with several names, check the beginning of the volume, which contains a rating of most attorneys: "av" signifies the highest calibre. Select an attorney and arrange for an initial consultation. There should be no charge for this, or at most a minimal one. Discuss with your lawyer whether or not you have a genuine case; courts have become much more strict in penalizing frivolous lawsuits with stiff fines or other sanctions.

SUCCESSFUL SUITS

Several types of violations of your civil liberties give good grounds for successful lawsuits. The overriding consideration is that you or your organization must *personally* have suffered the infringement. (Gloria

Estefan can't sue because Luther Campbell's rights have been violated; record stores can't sue if the state is discriminating only against video emporiums.)

Actual cases that have been fought are surprisingly diverse. For instance, in *Cinevision v. City of Burbank*, a federal appeals court recognized that rock fans and artists have a First Amendment right of access to government-owned concert facilities. The court refused to allow Burbank's city council to ban from the city-owned Starlight Bowl amphitheater performers, including Patti Smith and Jackson Browne, whom the council had described as "heavy metal bands, homosexuals and anti-nuclear activists." Just as important, the court made each city councilman *personally* pay punitive damages. The *Cinevision* decision is perhaps the most devastating legal precedent facing government censors today, because it threatens their personal pocketbooks. Unfortunately, few private attorneys — or government lawyers — seem to be inspired by its clear declaration. How else can you explain former San Antonio, Texas, mayor Henry Cisneros and city councilman Cameron Cosgrove of Irvine, California, making bans on heavy metal shows part of their political platform — and getting away with it?

Rock fans have also successfully sued against the pat-down searches often performed at the entrances of government-owned arenas. *Every one* of the eight U.S. appeals courts have declared these searches illegal under the Fourth Amendment protections against unreasonable searches and seizures. So has every state court that's tested it. And there are surely other unexploited favorable precedents applying to other areas of free speech.

WANTED: PATIENCE AND DEEP POCKETS

If your case has merit and you find a lawyer to handle it, don't expect results overnight. The legal process is long and slow by nature. But if you're successful — either in gaining a courtroom verdict or in an out-of-court settlement — you might have won not only an anti-censorship victory but money, too.

As your lawyer may tell you, another benefit to victorious civil liberties plaintiffs is that federal law permits you to be awarded attorneys' fees. In most other civil cases, you pay your lawyer out of whatever you win and are stuck with the expense if you lose.

Understanding that part is important, because fighting a civil liberties case is expensive, even with the assistance of groups like the ACLU, which does its legal work *pro bono* (for free). Your lawyer may be willing to work for a "contingent fee," meaning he or she only gets paid if you win. Or your lawyer may be willing to contribute his services because of the important issues involved. But other expenses — photocopying, research, court stenographers to write down everything said during depositions — add up quickly. Be prepared to stage some serious fund-raisers if you go this route.

But don't let these realities totally discourage you: Much of what the censors do is so blatantly unconstitutional that they'll be forced to settle with you — by giving you money and agreeing to knock it off —before the case reaches trial.

48
Have a Moment of Silence to Keep Speech Free

Help organize a symbolic "moment of silence" at bookstores, record stores, video stores, libraries, art galleries and museums, on radio and TV, and in the classroom. If our culture shuts down — for a minute, or preferably, for an hour or a day — then everyone will get a clearer picture of what would happen if the censors were ever to succeed in shutting us up.

A Day Without Art

"A Day Without Art" is an event produced by Visual AIDS, a volunteer group formed by members of the arts, crafts, design, press, and fashion communities. The aim of A Day Without Art is to raise awareness about AIDS, and to demand better health care and funding for research to help find a cure. A Day Without Art was also formed to "celebrate the achievements and lives of colleagues and friends while mourning the losses sustained." The event features exhibitions, readings, lectures, memorials, panel discussions, closings, cancellations of performances, removal of art, moments of silence, and advocacy and lobbying efforts.

The event, which began in 1989, takes place on December 1, the World Health Organization's annual AIDS Awareness Day. Nearly a thousand organizations, groups, and institutions participated in the 1989 event.

Many of A Day Without Art's ideas can be adapted by anti-censorship groups. This is appropriate, since the communities most affected by AIDS are among those most often censored, and since AIDS information itself is often distorted and embargoed by the same people who censor artists and journalists. Indeed, just before the 1989 event, the National Endowment for the Arts announced that it was rescinding a grant given to Artists Space, a non-profit organization in Manhattan, for its AIDS-related exhibit, *Witnesses: Against Our Vanishing*.

Contact Visual AIDS at 108 Leonard Street, 13th Floor, New York, NY 10013; (212) 513-0303.

49
Organize a Speak Out Day

Stage "Speak Out Day" in your city, featuring an anti-censorship parade. Dress up as characters from banned books, plays, and movies, sing banned songs, carry signs with the names of famous censored artists, carry urns containing symbolic ashes of burned books.

Why in the World Would You Wanna Do *That*?

Plato thought drama decadent — like every other social ritual that allowed the trading of souls. The censors have attacked the arts for much the same reason. Hit 'em in the breadbasket — stage a bacchanal, a festival that celebrates all the stuff they want us to believe that "normal" people would be ashamed to embrace. Take the show on the road. Get the dirty art out in the open so it can breathe again, and so ordinary folks can get a handle on it as something close-to-familiar, and nothing to fear. Besides, a festival is a way to turn the too-often-gloomy activity of First Amendment freedom-fighting into a helluva lot of fun.

Can You Really Do That Kinda Thing Around Here?

You *will* have to apply to your local police department for a parade permit. Be sure to apply far in advance, so no excuses can be made to deny your permit. (Apply in May or June for a September Banned Books Week anti-censorship parade.)

Remember: It is your *right* to demonstrate. To deny you a permit, the police must prove a threat of violence and disorder that jeopardizes public safety. If they decide to take away the key civil right to peacefully assemble — Sue! (See #47.)

Once you've received your permit, other local agencies can be very helpful. Work closely with the parks department and other city agencies. They're probably more experienced than you are, so ask them what they do on Memorial Day and Thanksgiving, then adapt their ideas to suit your purpose.

You will, in any event, need to be extremely well organized. A certain amount of chaos ought to characterize the event, perhaps. (Much creativity can spring forth from a little chaos.) But you need to give everybody a general sense of what they're doing and when to do it.

You're probably going to follow a standard parade route — down one of the main avenues of your town to a public park or square where you can have a rally. Try to strike a balance in the floats and exhibits between education and entertainment and silliness. Too much "educating" and you're preaching; too much "entertaining," and your audience won't get the point, which is that free speech is both precious and in grave danger.

The great thing about a parade is that you can educate bystanders along the parade route. That's why the rally needs to be at the *end* of the parade route rather than at the beginning. That's why all the entertainment and silliness is indispensable — you'll seem to be a great bunch to hang out with, and at the same time, you'll let the air out of the censors' gasbags.

Recipe for a Parade

• Stage fantasy encounters of the free speech kind: Dress up as a chainsmoking Edward R. Murrow and interrogate a sweating, porcine Joe McCarthy. Or dress a crew as priggish pseudo scholars and set them to watching dirty pictures, on a float called "The Meese Commission."

• Set Huck and Jim on the back of a pickup truck, grooving to "Fight the Power."

• Ask local bands — from schools or other groups — to participate and expand their repertoire with censored songs. And form your own group: A hundred and one kazoos playing a medley of "Me So Horny," "Louie Louie," and "We Shall Overcome" would sound great.

• Carry huge blowups of the faces of banned artists: Henry Miller, Karen Finley, William Burroughs, James Joyce, John Lennon, Robert Mapplethorpe, Anne Frank, James Baldwin, Richard Wright, D.H. Lawrence.

• Some of the best floats are based on fairy tales. In your parade, you can dress as characters that illustrate censorship myths and legends. How about a guitar player with his mouth held closed by a record label, to illustrate the fable that record labels aren't censorship? Dress another person up as Mapplethorpe's black man in a polyester suit. Set Jesus dancing with the Beatles on the back of a flatbed truck — the Beatles should be bigger than Jesus, of course.

• Stage a series of dramatic readings from banned books. End the day with a reading of Molly Bloom's soliloquy from Joyce's *Ulysses*.

• If you're not gonna do your own parade, at least put a First Amendment float in other local parades. The Missoula, Montana, library put a "Big Banned Books" float in a University of Montana homecoming parade whose theme was "The Big Band Era."

50
Make the Real Obscenities the Real Issues

Attack the real obscenities: Homelessness, unemployment, war and militarism, racism, sexism, AIDS, homophobia. Make alliances with groups working on these issues.

Censorship often serves the basic purpose of thought control. It's designed to distract public attention from massive budget boondoggles, urban decay, poverty, the government's failure to solve problems while entire communities starve amidst "prosperity." It's designed to sweep aside essential questions — about power and its profits, particularly —while raising phony ones. It serves to keep people who might otherwise

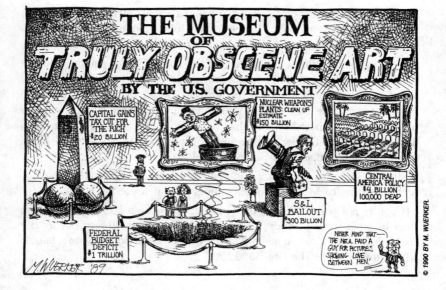

be raising such issues, proposing inconvenient solutions, and taking action, constantly on the defensive, battling for the basic right to say anything at all.

Two can play this game. Steamroller the polite boundaries of mutual "civilized" understandings about "the reasonable limits of free speech." Be impatient and make it clear you feel the entire argument for censorship is frivolous, and should be dropped — that is, resolved in favor of *letting people speak*, so that more urgent issues can be addressed.

Remember: It is *obvious* that *any* limits on free speech are unconstitutional. You're entitled to be abrupt and disruptive when entire areas of national debate get bogged down by censorship issues.

Censors are often drawn to the big noise. Their goal is to cover up its real source. Don't let them distract you:

• 3,000,000 Americans are homeless;

• 13 percent of the country is only one paycheck from the street;

- 10 percent of the country is going to bed hungry;
- 1,175 Americans die from AIDS every week;
- Every 18 seconds a man batters a woman in her own home;
- The estimated cost of cleaning up the nuclear waste generated by military weapons is $200 billion;
- One in five adults is functionally illiterate;
- Black family median income is 57 percent of white family income;
- Nearly 20 percent of all children in the United States live below the poverty level;
- Over 58,000 Americans and nearly two million Vietnamese died in Vietnam, and more than 100,000 died in the 43 -day war in the Middle East.

These are the concrete realities the censors don't talk about. And these are the problems that merit anything we can do to solve them.

Never forget: The active use of your freedom of speech is a position of power — a base from which you can affect other issues.

How?

Make it clear you realize that, to some, silence is a welcome substitute for the raw, the obsessive, and the foreign, but that it is not the road to understanding.

Declare that it's your duty to speak out for those without a voice —Bob Dylan's "countless confused, accused, misused, strung-out ones and worse." In this way, make it clear that witnessing for another is not only your privilege but your right.

As censors try to narrow the issue past the point of absurdity, continue to broaden the terrain until it reflects all aspects of reality.

Do not allow the drama to descend to a shouting match. When freedom of speech is on trial, make it clear that the issue is not merely whether you can fondle your genitals on stage, but also whether we can openly say that the arms race is a similar gesture, involving more respectable men playing with larger phalluses.

Ask for a moment of silence for those who died speaking out.

AFTERWORD

There are different kinds of people who fight censorship. I think of myself as sort of a designated hitter for those anti-censorship people who are not artists, who are not writers or academics, but who benefit from those people and who support those people.

In short, we are bona fide members of the capitalist class, strictly small-time capitalists, people who run art galleries, bookstores, print shops, small book publishers. All of us are entrepreneurs. And we have advantages. We have a certain flexibility. We even have the ability to act freely when action is necessary. And we're responsible to ourselves, our creative people, and our pocketbooks. Not to our government or anyone else.

In my case I came equipped with a certain built-in objection to higher authority. Whether it was my private idea of the Catholic Church or the Jewish social hierarchy or the Chicago police, or the eighth grade, Chicago gave to me, Irish-Jewish renegade, an awful lot of great targets to go after.

But equally important, or more important from these same sources like James Ferrell, Studs Lonigan, Nelson Algren's *Neon Wilderness*, and Meyer Levin's *The Old Bunch*, from them I got a very strong idea of what was right and wrong, and keeping human beings from reaching their potential was the real pits, the real wipeout. Full potential meant to me having freedom of speech in all the nuances of that wonderful phrase.

While I was a freshman at Swarthmore College in 1940, a place which I considered to be the world center of stultification, I somehow found or the book found me, at Frances Stoloff's Gotham Book Mart, on 47th Street in New York City, the book *Tropic of Cancer* by Henry Miller. And then I even wrote my freshman term paper on the book. And my benign professor wrote on my paper that the jaundice is in the eye of the beholder. Meaning, I guess, that for Miller and me, our feeling about the United States was somehow sick.

Oddly, I don't even remember the erotic content as having been important. It was the attack on the establishment that bowled me over. The other subject matter was quite forcibly brought to my attention later, and I welcomed it. After all, I was a struggling capitalist.

Some years after that, having exhausted my GI bill on all the literature courses offered at the New School in New York, I sort of tripped into publishing. Henry Miller was still part of my baggage, my backpack. And censorship was becoming even more irksome to me. So I created my own Tinkers to Evers to Chance publishing combination, which became Herman Melville to Henry James to D.H. Lawrence.

And after that setup clicked, our cleanup hitter appeared, Henry Miller and *Tropic of Cancer*. I'd waited a long time. Everything did not happen the way I'd foreseen. The vision wasn't that clear. I didn't know that one day the *Evergreen Review* offices would be bombed and the wonderful portrait of Che Guevara done by Paul Davis would be stabbed in the office. But we survived that, too. And as somebody who in the eighth grade put out a paper called *Anti-Everything*, from there to *Tropic of Cancer* was a fairly straight, even logical course.

Small entrepreneurs have been the pursuers of dreams *and* revolutionary ideas. But they also have a sensible streak. Otherwise they'd starve to death. (And some of them do.) But it is the artists, the writers, the creative people who give us entrepreneurs our reason for being. In turn, we, their publishers, are their protectors and guardians. And that is our function. We are in effect the foot soldiers in the struggle against hypocrisy and oppression.

— BARNEY ROSSET
1990

INDEX

Accuracy in Academia, 108
Accuracy in Media, 20
Address to the German Nobility, 37
Age of Reason, The, 37
AIDS crisis, 76, 112, 115, 117
ALA Journal, The, 59
Alexander, Danny, 26, 106-107
Algren, Nelson, 118
Alice's Adventures in Wonderland, 37
Amen Corner, 22
America, 79
American Association of University Professors
    (AAUP), 108
American Bar Association (ABA), 105
American Booksellers Association, 23, 64
American Broadcasting Co. (ABC), 17, 55, 84
American Civil Liberties Union (ACLU), xviii,
    22, 47, 57-58, 110-111
American Family Association (AFA), 51, 65,
    66-67, 69, 108
American Federation of the Arts, 62-63
American Heritage Dictionary, 37
American Libraries, 59
American Library Association (ALA), 1, 15,
    22, 23-24, 37, 59, 73, 96, 100, 104, 106
American Medical Association (AMA), 29
American Pediatric Association, 67
American Society of Journalists and Authors,
    23, 25
American Telephone & Telegraph (AT&T), 70
Amusing Ourselves to Death, 21
"Annie Had a Baby," 44
Anti-Censorship Songs, List of Ten Great, 46
Are You There God? It's Me, Margaret, 15
Aristotle, 62
Arms, Karen, 38
Arnett, Peter, xvii
Art Censorship, 60
Article 19, 63
As I Lay Dying, 37
As Nasty As They Wanna Be, 45
Association of American Publishers, 23
Authors League of America, 37

Back in Control Training Center, 68
Bagdikian, Ben, 19
Baker, James, 65, 67, 72
Baker, Susan, 66, 67, 72
Baldwin, James, 22, 39, 115

Baldwin, Roger, 58
Ballard, Hank, 44
Bandinelli, Baccio, 62
Banned Art, List of, 60-63
Banned Books Week, 15, 23-24, 25, 37, 91,
    113
Banned Books Week Resource Book, The, 15,
    96, 104
Banned Books, List of Fifty Great, 37-41
Banned Films, 100
"Banned in the U.S.A.," 46
Barefoot Channel, The, 57, 102
BAUhaus Arts Center, 98
Beastie Boys, The, 46
Beatles, The, 45, 68, 115
Beggar's Banquet, 45
Bell Jar, The, 37
Bernard, James, 29
BET, 56
"Beyond the Realms of Death," 45
Biafra, Jello, 36, 44
Bible, The, 43, 108
Big Book of Kids' List, The, 15
Bill of Rights, 11, 22
Biology, 38
Birdbrain, 81
Birth of a Nation, The, 99
Blake, William, 81
Bloom, Allan, 106
Bloom, Molly, 15
Blume, Judy, 15
Bob Larson's Ministries, 68
*Bookbanning in America: Who Bans Books and
    Why*, 36
Bookstore Chains, List of Major, 34
Boston Women's Health Book Collective, 15,
    40
Bradley, Bill
Brave New World, 38
Brecht, Bertolt, 44
Broadcasting, 53
"Brown Eyed Girl," 46
Browne, Jackson, 111
Bruce, Tammy, 69
Bryan, William Jennings, 57
Buckley, William, 70
Burbank, CA, 111
Burger King 67, 85
Burgess, Anthony, 22, 38

Burroughs, William, 40, 80, 115
Business Week, 92

Cable News Network (CNN), xvii, 19, 27
Cable Television and the First Amendment, 57, 103
Cable Television, 103
Calhoun Country, AL, 22
Camp, Pamela S., 38
Can Control, 42
Candide, 38
Cantwell, David, 26, 105-107
Caravaggio, 62
Carnal Knowledge, 100
Carroll, Lewis, 37
Carter, Jimmy, 19
Catch-22, 38
Catcher in the Rye, The, 38, 106
Censor's Greatest Hits, List of the, 44-46
Censorship and Selection: Issues and Answers for Schools, 75, 107, 109
Censorship or Selection, 75, 102
Center for Arts Advocacy, 42, 89
Center for Civic Education, The, 28, 74, 105, 108-109
Center for War, Peace and the News Media, 20
Central Park SummerStage, 98
Chap's on Main, 98
Charlie and the Chocolate Factory, 38
Chicago Artists' Coalition/Committee for Artists' Rights, 94
Chicago Heights, IL, 51
Child Protection Obscenity Enforcement Act, 66
Christian Leaders for Responsible Television (CLeaR-TV), 66, 67, 85
Christine, 22
Cincinnati, OH, 8
Cinderella, 74
Cinevision v. City of Burbank, 111
Cisneros, Henry, 111
Citizens for Excellence in Education (CEE), 74
Clinton, George, 46
Clockwork Orange, A, 22, 38
Closing of the American Mind, 106
Cloward, Richard A., 87
Club MTV, 54
Coalition of Writers Organizations, The (COWO), 35
Coasters, The, 46
Color Purple, The, 22
Columbia Broadcasting System (CBS), 55, 66, 67

Columbia Journalism Review, 20
Columbia Pictures, 50
Communications Consortium, 20
Communism, Hypnotism, and the Beatles, 68
Complete Home Video Book The, 83
Concerned Women of America, 74
Congressional Quarterly Weekly Report, The, 13
Congressional Voting Guide, The, 13
Constitutional Rights Foundation, The, 105
Cosgrove, Cameron, 111
Countering the Conspiracy to Destroy Black Boys, 23
Creationism, 73, 108
"Crossfire", 19
Crusades, The, 74
Cry Baby, 100

Daddy Was a Number Runner, 38
Dahl, Roald, 38
Dante, 39
Darrow, Clarence, 57
Darwinian evolution, 73
Davis, Bette, 100
Davis, Jim, 38
Davis, Paul, 119
Day, Doris, 22
Day Without Art, A, 112-113
Days of Rage, 70
De Palma, Brian, 47
Deadline, 20
Declaration of Independence, 38
Delaware Valley Anti-Censorship Coalition, 94
Desktop Video, 83
Dialogue Concerning the Two Chief World Systems, 39
Diary of Anne Frank, The, 15, 39, 74
Dickens, Charles, 40
Directing Video, 83
Divine Comedy, The, 39
Dixon, Jean, 76-78
Dobson, Dr. James, 49, 66
Dolce, Joe, 46,
Doyle, Sir Arthur Conan, 15, 37
Dylan, Bob, 45, 68, 81, 117

Eagle Forum, 66, 67-68, 74
Education Research Analysts, 73
Eicher, Ben, 110
Elk Grove Village, IL, 51
Ellison, Ralph, 39
Entertainment Weekly, 53
Equal Rights Amendment, 67, 74

Essential Information, 20
Evergreen Review, 118
"Everyday People," 46
Exorcist, The, 100
Extra!, 19-20

Fahrenheit 451, 100
Fairness and Accuracy in Reporting (FAIR), 19-20
Family Circle, 84
Faulkner, William, 37
Faust, 39
Federal Communications Commission (FCC), 43, 55, 56, 79, 81, 102
Ferrell, James, 118
"Fight For Your Right To Party," 46
Finley, Karen, 115
"Firing Line," 20, 70
First Amendment, xvii, 1, 2, 3, 11, 12, 16, 24, 25, 27, 35, 48, 56, 58, 60, 72, 74, 75, 76, 87, 88, 89, 90, 91, 94, 96, 99, 104, 106, 110, 111, 113, 115
Fitzgerald, F. Scott, 39
Flaubert, Gustave, 39
Focus on the Family, 28, 49, 65-66, 67, 69, 108
Focus on the Family Citizen, 66
Folk Music and the Negro Revolution, 68
Fort Lauderdale, FL, 8
Foundation for Free Expression, ABA, 64
Fourth Amendment, 111
Frank, Anne, 15, 38, 115
Freedom to Read Foundation, 59
Freedom to Read Foundation News, 59
Freedom Writer, The, 36
"---- Tha Police," 45, 66

Gabler, Mel, 73-74
Gabler, Norma, 73-74
Galilei, Galileo, 39, 106
Garbage Pail Kids, 66
Garfield: His Nine Lives, 38
Gauntlet, The, 35, 42
Genet, Jean, 80
Ginsberg, Allen, 39, 43, 79-81
GlobalVision, 70
Go Ask Alice, 39
"God Save the Queen," 45
Goethe, Johann Wolfgang von, 39
"Goodnight Irene," 45
Gore, Jr., Albert, 8, 67
Gore, Tipper, 66, 67, 68
Gotham Book Mart, 118

Gould, Stephen Jay, 73
Granda, Michael "Supe", 76-77
Great Gatsby, The, 39
Greater Kansas City Coalition Against Censorship, The, 98
Greenberg, David, 41
Griffin, Carol, 67
Groening, Matt, 52
Group for Rap Industry Protection (GRIP), 42
Guevara, Che, 118
Guide of the Perplexed, 39

Hair Spray, 100
Hall, Karen, 83-86
Happy Prince and Other Stories, The, 39
Heller, Joseph, 38
Helms, Jesse, 66, 79, 80, 81, 91, 93
Heritage Foundation, 79, 80
"Hill Street Blues," 85
Hitler, Adolf, 29, 40
Hoffman, Harry, 64
Hollywood Reporter, 53
Holm, Bill, 79-80
Holocaust, The, 74
Home Box Office (HBO), 54
Home Dish Only Satellite Network, 56
Homer, 40
How to Develop a Voter Registration Plan, 88
How to Register Voters at a Central Site, 88
Howl, 39, 43, 79, 80, 81
Huckleberry Finn, The Adventures of, 15, 16, 22, 83, 114
Hughes, Langston, 38
Hussein, Saddam, 29
Huxley, Aldous, 38

"I Wanna Testify," 46
Ice-T, 44
If Beale Street Could Talk, 22, 39
Illinois Coalition Against Censorship, 12
"Imagine," 46
Independent Film Importers and Distributors Association, 48
Inherit the Wind, 72, 100
Intellectual Freedom Committee, ALA, 1
Internal Revenue Code, 71
Inventing Reality, 21
Invisible Man, 39
Irvine, CA, 111

J'accuse, 39
James, Henry, 118
JC Penney, 51

"Jesse Don't Like It," 46
Jesus, 115
Jethro Tull, 46
Jordan, Michael, 53
Joyce, James, 41, 50, 115
Judas Priest, 45
Justice, U.S. Department of, 92

Kaddish, 79, 81
Kafka, Franz, 48
Kaufman, Philip, 47
Kazantzakis, Nikos, 40
"Kick Out the Jams, Motherfuckers," 44
King Arthur, 74
King of May, 81
King, Larry, 22, 30
King, Martin Luther, 68
King, Stephen, 22, 41
Kingsmen, The, 45
Kinsley, Michael, 19
Kissinger, Henry, 19
Kollwitz, Kathe, 62
Kondrake, Morton, 70
Koppel, Ted, 19
Kral Majales, 79
Kramer, Larry, 76
Kunjufu, Jawanza, 23
"Kwitny Report, The," 20, 70
Kwitny, Jonathan, 70

"L.A. Law," 85
Lady Chatterley's Lover, 40
LaHaye, Beverly, 74
Larson, Bob, 68
Last Temptation of Christ, The, 40, 66, 100
Lawrence, D.H., 40, 79, 80, 115, 118
League of Women Voters, 10
Leaves of Grass, 40
Lee, Harper, 15, 41
Lenin, Vladimir I., 38
Lennon, John, 45, 46, 115
"Let's Spend the Night Together," 46
Levin, Meyer, 118
Liberty Denied, 36
Lies of Our Times, 21
"Like A Prayer," 45, 66
"Live to Tell," 46
"Locomotive Breath," 46
Loder, Kurt, 53
Lonigan, Studs, 118
Looking-Glass World of Non-Fiction TV, The, 21
Lorax, The, 22

"Louie Louie," 45, 114
Luther, Martin, 37
Lynn, Barry, xviii

"M*A*S*H," 85
MacMonnies, Frederick, 62
"MacNeil/Lehrer News Hour," 70
Madame Bovary, 39
Madison, WI, 23
Madonna, xvii, 45, 46, 55, 56, 66
Maimonides, 39
Manet, Edouard, 62
Manufacturing Consent, 21
Mapplethorpe, Robert, xvii, 8, 27, 115
Marquez, Gabriel Garcia, 40
"Married with Children," 70
Marsh, Dave, 36
Marvin, Shirley, 67
Marxist Minstrels, The, 68
Mazrui, Ali, 3
McCarthy, Joe, 114
Media Alliance, 21
"Media Brokers: Concentration and Ownership of the Press, The," 19
Media Monopoly, The, 21
Meese Commission, 114
Mein Kampf, 40
Melville, Herman, 118
Meriwether, Louise, 38
"Me So Horny," 114
MGM/Pathé, 49
Michelangelo, 62
Michigan Council on the Arts, 70
Middle East, xvii, 117
Mighty Mouse, 66
Miller, Henry, 22, 41, 80, 115, 118
Miller, Jim, 40-41
Mismeasure of Man, The, 73
Missoula, MT, 115
Missouri Project Rock (MPR), 67
Montgomery (AL) bus boycott, 73
Moral Majority, 74, 85, 92
Morality in Media
Morello, Mary, 16, 94-95
Morrison, Jim, 45
Morrison, Van, 46
Morrow, Edward R., 64, 114
Mother Goose: Old Nursery Rhymes, 40
Motion Picture Association of America (MPAA), 47, 49
"Mr. Belvedere," 85
MTV, 53-54, 55
Multinational Monitor, 19

Murdoch, Rupert, 53
Murphy, Barbara Beasley, 22
Music in Action, 92
Music Retail Chains, List of Major, 32-34

N.W.A., 45
Nader, Ralph, 30
Naked Lunch, 39
National Association of Broadcasters, 55
National Association of Christian Educators, 74
National Association of College Stores, 23
National Association of Theatre Owners, 48
National Broadcasting Co. (NBC), 55
National Cable Televison Assoc., 55
National Campaign for Freedom of Expression, 60
National Coalition Against Censorship, 25-26
National Coalition on Television Violence (NCTV), 51, 70
National Endowment for the Arts (NEA), 11, 60, 66, 113
National Federation of Decency (NFD), 66
National Institute for Citizen Education in the Law, The, 105
National Organization for Women (NOW), 69
National Public Radio, 19
Nazis, American, 57
NC-17 movie rating, 27, 47-49, 50
Negro Writers, The Best Short Stories by, 38
Neon Wilderness, 118
Network Broadcast Standards, 84
New Age religion, 73
New Democratic Party, Ontario, 17
New Republic, The, 19
New School, The, 118
New York Times, The, 17, 70
New York Times Magazine, The, 66
Newsletter on Intellectual Freedom, The, 24, 35, 95
Newsweek, 2
Nielsen Co., A.C., 107
"Nightline," 119
Nike, 53
1984, 40, 100
Nixon, Richard, 45, 52
No More Censorship Defense Fund (NMCDF), 36, 43, 44, 74
Noebel, David, 68
Noriega, Manuel, 27
Normal Heart, The, 76

Odyssey, The, 40
Office of Intellectual Freedom, ALA, 15, 22,

Old Bunch, The, 118
Oliver Twist, 40
Onassis, Jacqueline Kennedy, 23
One Hundred Years of Solitude, 40
Origin of the Species, On the, 40
Orion Pictures, 49
Orwell, George, 40, 48, 79
Osbourne, Ozzy, 45
Our Bodies, Ourselves, 15, 40
Ozark Mountain Daredevils, 76

Pacifica Radio Network, 19, 79
Paine, Thomas, 37
Paramount Communications, 49
Parent Teacher Association (PTA), 44, 69-70
Parents for Rock and Rap, 16, 94
Parents' Music Resource Center (PMRC), 8, 28, 65, 66, 67, 68
Parks, Rosa, 73
P.E.N. International, 122
PEN American Center, 37
PEN Center U.S.A. West, 37
People Like Us, 25
Peters, Dan, 68
Peters, Steve, 68
Pharoahs, The, 74
Phyllis Schlafly Report, 67-68
Pilgrims, The, 74
Pink Flamingos, 100
Pittston (VA) strike, 29
Piven, Frances Fox, 87
Plath, Sylvia, 37
Plato, 60
Presley, Elvis, 45, 52
Price, Lloyd, 46
Producer's Sourcebook, 103
Project Vote, 88-89
Propaganda Review, 21
Public Broadcasting System, 52, 70

Rackman, Arthur, 40
Radecki, Thomas, 70
Radical Media, 21
"Rainy Day Women #13 & 35," 45
Raising PG Kids in an X-Rated World, 66
Rakolta, Terry, 70
Rambo, 70
Reagan, Ronald, 87
Real Art Ways, 98
Real Frank Zappa Book, The, 36
Rhythm, Riots and Revolution, 68
Robertson, Rev. Pat, 69
Robinson, Phil Alden, 47
Rock & Roll Confidential, 36, 42, 43, 95

Rock Out Censorship, 5
Rock The Vote! (RTV), 88
Rodin, August, 62
Rohrbacher, Dana, 93
Rolling Stone Illustrated History of Rock and Roll 1950-1980, 40-41
Rolling Stones, The, 45, 46, 78
Rosset, Barney, 118-119
Run-D.M.C., 46
Rushdie, Salman, xvii, 27, 41

Salinger, J.D., 38
Samuel Goldwyn Co., The, 49
San Antonio, TX, 67, 111
San Francisco Arts Democratic Club, 89
Sanders, Bernie, 19
Satanic Verses, The, 27, 41
Sawyer, Diane, 19
Schlafly, Phyllis, 66, 67, 74
Scopes trial, 57
Scorsese, Martin, 47, 66
Seals and Crofts, 68
Seuss, Dr., 22
700 Club, 69
Seven Minutes, The, 100
Sex Pistols, The, 45
"Shaddap You Face," 46
Sherlock Holmes, the Adventures of, 15, 37
Shining, The, 41
Shostakovich, Dmitri, 45
Sign of the Times, A, 26-28, 105
Simpson, Bart, 16, 51, 52
"Simpsons, The," 16, 51-52
Sinatra, Frank, 78
Skokie, IL, 57
Slugs, 41
Sly and the Family Stone, 46
Small Format Television Production, 83
Smith, Patti, 111
Song of Solomon, The, 43
Source, The, 29, 36
"South Africa Now," 20, 70
Speaker, The, 100
Speaking and Writing the Truth: Community Forums on the First Amendment, 105
Springfield, MO, 76-78
Springsteen, Bruce, 44, 67
"Stagger Lee," 46
Star of David, 68
Starlight Bowl, 111
Steinbeck, John, 22
Stoloff, Frances, 118
Storm Center, 100

"Suicide Solution," 45
Summit Ministries, 68
Sunflower Sutra, 79, 81
Supreme Court, The U.S., 43
Swarthmore College, 118

Teicher, Oren, 64
Tell It to the King, 22
Ten Commandments for the Fight Against Censorship, 2-4
Thompson, Gov. James, 12
Thompson, Jack, 4, 67
Threepenny Opera, The, 44
Time-Warner, 53
To Kill a Mockingbird, 15, 41
"Tom & Jerry," 70
Toughlove, 85
Tracy, Spencer, 100
Tropic of Cancer, 41, 118, 119
Trumpet to Arms, A, 21
Truth About Rock Ministries, 68
Turner, Tina, 68
TV Guide, 53, 70
Twain, Mark, 15
Twentieth Century Fox, 49, 52, 55
21st Century Film, 49
2 Live Crew, 4, 8, 27, 45, 46, 67
"Tzena Tzena Tzena," 45

Ulysses, 41, 115
U.S. Constitution Bicentennial, 36
United Nations, 62
Universal Delaration of Human Rights, UN, 62
Universal Pictures, 49, 66
Unreliable Sources, 21

Valenti, Jack, 47, 49
Variety, 53
Variety Sourcebook, 103
Veronese, 62
Video Production Guide, The, 83
Video Retailers, List of, 34-35
Video Review, 82
Video Source Book, The, 102
Visual AIDS, 112-113
Voltaire, Francois, 38
Voter Registration Information Lines, 9
Voting Rights Act, 68

Wainwright III, Loudon, 46
Walden Book Co., 64
Walesa, Lech, 29
"Walk This Way," 46

Walker, Alice, 22
Walsh, Sheila, 69
Walt Disney Co., 49
Warner Communications, Inc., 49
Washington Coalition Against Censorship, 94
Watergate scandal, 73
Waters, John, 100
Weavers, The, 45
Webster's Ninth New Collegiate Dictionary, 15
"Week in Rock, The," 54
Weill, Kurt, 44
"We Shall Overcome," 114
Whitman, Walt, 40, 80, 81
Why Knock Rock, 68
Wilde, Oscar, 39
Wildmon, Rev. Donald, 66, 85
Williams, Jerry, 30
Williams, William Carlos, 81
Winning America, 21
Wizard of Oz, The, 74
Wojnarowicz, David, 66

Women Against Pornography (WAP), 69
Working with Video, 83
World Health Organization, 112
WRKO-AM (Boston), 30
Wright, Richard, 115

X-rating, movies, 47-48, 50

"Yakety Yak," 46
Yard, Molly, 69
Yesterday and Today, 45
"Yo, MTV Raps," 54
You've Got a Right To Rock, 36, 43
Young, Art, 62

Z-PAC, 36
Zappa, Frank, 36
Zermuehlen, Don, 23
Zola, Emile, 39
Zoom Black Magic, 44, 102

DAVE MARSH has been writing and lecturing about censorship since the early 1980s. Marsh is the author of more than a dozen books about popular music, including two best-sellers about Bruce Springsteen, *Born to Run* and *Glory Days*. He edited the first two editions of *The Rolling Stone Record Guide*, as well as *Pastures of Plenty*, from the papers of folksinger Woody Guthrie. A founder of *Creem*, former associate editor of *Rolling Stone*, and a current music critic for *Playboy*, Marsh also edits *Rock & Roll Confidential*, a newsletter about music and politics, with a special emphasis on censorship. For the past several years he has lectured on music censorship at campuses around the United States.

Marsh lives in New York City and Connecticut with his wife and two daughters. He serves on the board of the Rhythm and Blues Foundation and the advisory board of National Writers Union.

GEORGE PLIMPTON is editor of the *Paris Review*, the literary quarterly which he founded in 1953. He is the author of numerous magazine articles and books — including the best-selling *Paper Lion* — and selections from his work have been collected in the recently published book, *The Best of Plimpton*. While conducting research for his writings, Plimpton has (among other things) played quarterback for the Detroit Lions, basketball with the Boston Celtics, percussion with the New York Philharmonic, and has flown on a trapeze for the Clyde Beatty-Cole Brothers Circus.

BARNEY ROSSET was the editor and publisher of Grove Press from 1951 to 1986. In 1957 he published D.H. Lawrence's *Lady Chatterly's Lover*, winning a battle against censors in what became a landmark court case, and paved the way for Grove's publication of such banned and controversial books as *Tropic of Cancer*, *Naked Lunch*, *Last Exit to Brooklyn*, *The Autobiography of Malcolm X*, and *The Wretched of the Earth*. In 1987 Rosset founded Blue Moon Books. In 1988 he received the PEN citation "for continuous service to International Letters, to the Freedom and Dignity of writers, and to the Free Transmission of the Printed Word, Across Barriers of Poverty, Ignorance, Censorship and Repression."